The
Plastic
Modeller's
Handbook

THE PLASTIC MODELLER'S HANDBOOK

EDITED BY KELVIN BARBER

ARGUS BOOKS

Argus Books Limited
Wolsey House
Wolsey Road
Hemel Hempstead
Hertfordshire HP2 4SS

First published by Argus Books 1989

ISBN 0 85242 970 3

Photosetting by Gilbert Composing Services, Leighton Buzzard.
Printed and bound by LR Printing Services Ltd.
Manor Royal, Crawley, West Sussex, RH10 2QN, England.

CONTENTS

FOREWORD

The Plastic Modeller's Handbook is a wide-ranging and comprehensive guide to all aspects of plastic models, with mention also being made of white metal and resin modelling. The book has been written by experts in all the various important aspects of the hobby and was commissioned to fill the increasing need for a fully up-to-date and accessible reference work on the hobby.

In the book, you will find essential, practical information on aircraft converting, high-tech kits, vacforms, dioramas, cars, ships, detailing, painting and accessories—in short, all you need to be a successful plastic modeller.

The authors are all regular contributors to 'Scale Models International' and, as such, are in day-to-day contact with modellers and model manufacturers throughout the world. *The Plastic Modeller's Handbook* encapsulates this knowledge and experience into one indispensible volume which we hope will take pride of place on your bookshelf.

Kelvin Barber
Editor 'Scale Models International'
February 1989

INTRODUCTION

MAT IRVINE

It is difficult to put a precise date on when the first modern commercial plastic construction kit appeared, or even who actually produced it, but it is generally accepted that the Gowland and Gowland series of car models has to be the favourite contender. If this is so, it means that this aspect of the hobby has to be nearing its 40th birthday! This isn't to say that

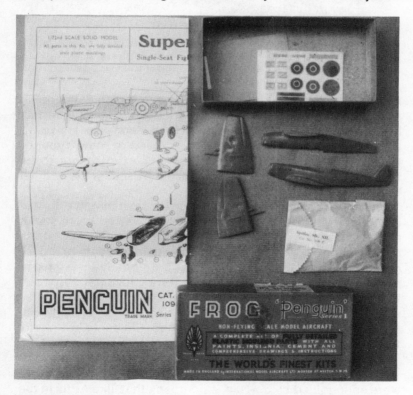

The first 'plastic construction kits'—the Frog Penguins—moulded not from polystyrene but cellulose acetate, a far less stable plastic and one that warps very easily. This kit is worth considerably more left unassembled as the result would hardly match those of today's standards.

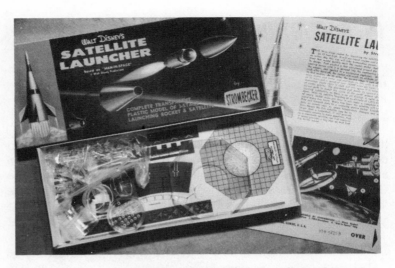

Even as long ago as the mid 50s, manufacturers were offering 'kits with a difference'. This rare Strombecker model from their 'Disney' series was moulded entirely in clear plastic, with a full-colour launching pad.

there were no model kits and modellers before this, and these new types of kits were not even the first 'plastic' kits, this honour going to the early pre-war Frog Penguins. However, what was different was that they used a new type of thermoplastic plastic—polystyrene—which turned out to be far superior to the earlier cellulose acetate used for the original kits.

This new plastic meant that far greater detail could be put into a mould and that the finished result was far more stable and retained its shape without warpage—the new age of the construction kit was born. Some companies, such as Monogram, Lindberg and Strombecker were already in existence and they modified their existing wooden kit lines to incorporate these new-fangled ideas. They were soon joined by names such as Aurora, Hawk and Revell—who worked closely with Gowland and Gowland in the United States—while Airfix began in Britain. In addition, companies such as AMT (Aluminum Model Toys), who began life making metal promotional cars, changed over to this new style of plastic and were soon joined by Jo-Han, a company that, like Airfix in the UK, became specialists in all forms of injection moulded plastic from plastic kitchen utensils, to plastic moulding for electric equipment, as well as these new style of construction kits.

All commercially moulded construction kits rely on the injection moulding machine, which is basically a large press that pushes liquified polystyrene into the steel tool under immense pressure. The polystyrene itself starts as granules to which can be added artificial rubber to vary the flexibility of the finished parts, a lubricant to assist flow and colouring pigments where necessary. The mould or tool into which the plastic is injected is cut from extremely hard steel, pantographed down from a larger pattern to retain detail, although final panel lines and the like are invariably hand cut after the main work is done automatically. The fit of the tool is vital as it will be subjected to many hundreds of tons pressure during the injection process. Any flaw will soon show up on the moulded parts with the most common being 'flash', the thin layer of plastic that shows where the tool halves did not fit as precisely as would be wished, and usually a sign of a mould that is wearing out.

The cutting of this steel tool is the most expensive part of any model kit and this obviously means that the maximum usage has to be got out of the mould by the model company. Original tooling tended to be cut directly into the steel of the main bulk, or perhaps as was the case with many of the original moulds into a berillium steel insert, which was extremely hard and

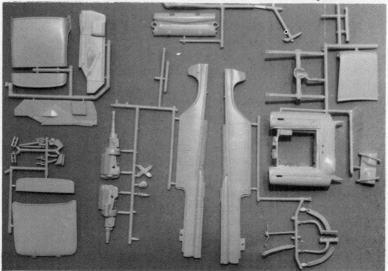

Not all larger scaled car kits had one-piece bodies. This multi-piece example is Revell's amazing Ford Fairlane Skyliner with its totally retractable hard-top.

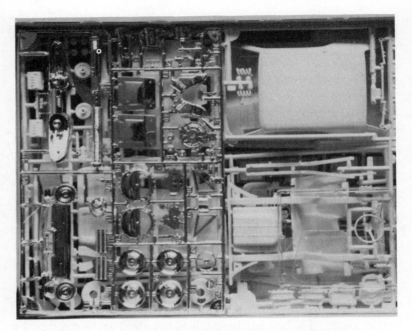

Packing kit parts in their boxes is not always as logical as this example from Jo-Han. This kit, their Crysler Turbine Car, shows how the kit runners are designed to stack upon each other.

became even more hardened under use. Nowadays, moulds tend to be made with numerous inserts for each part or set of parts. This means that, should one particular area become damaged for whatever reason, it can be replaced with a new insert. Older methods require a whole new block to be welded in and recut, which usually showed on the finished part. This method of inserts also means that the main tool can be modified or parts blanked off far more easily, thus getting more use from the basic shapes.

When the shape of the parts themselves are cut, the machinery also adds the flow channels for the molten plastic. The point where the plastic enters the part is the 'gate' and should be as thin as possible to eliminate too large an attachment area to the main run of plastic. This is always called the 'sprue' in the modelling fraternity, but what you get in the kit is not the sprue. This is actually the far larger run of plastic that leads to the mould in the first place and is never included with the kit—if it was, there wouldn't be room for the rest of the parts! The surround to the parts is actually the 'runner' and it is this that is utilised in the time-honoured method 'stretching sprue' to make aerials and rigging.

Quality control with all manufacturers is usually very high, but the odd fault can slip through. As mentioned, the most common fault is flash, but this usually indicates an old mould. There is no use taking the kit back to the shop and demanding a new one as they will all be the same. This has become more obvious recently with the number of reissued kits from old tooling being released, but this does give new builders a chance to construct some older, very desirable kits. For the sake of some flash, which is the easiest of faults to correct, most will agree it is worth the small amount of extra effort. Less easy to correct are 'short mouldings' where the plastic has not reached the full length of the mould, but these are very rare and are usually picked up long before the kit reaches the packing stage, when the whole batch will be rejected and probably recycled back into the raw material for new kits.

These days, kits are usually packed in bags inside their boxes, making the chance of a part being lost through examination in the shop extremely rare. However, note that this

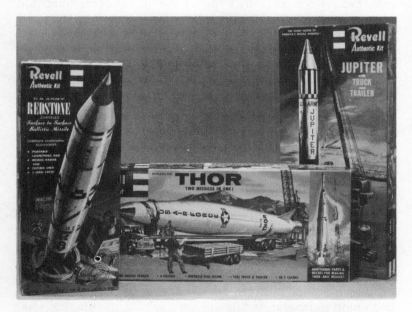

Some of Revell's highly sought-after 'S' series of kits from the late 50s/early 60s. Many were of missiles and some were reissued in the early 80s as 'History Makers' though with far less evocative box art.

usually only applies to the main parts themselves; the clear, chromed and possibly red or other translucent parts, along with the decal sheet and plans, are packed separately and can be lost. Many manufacturers are now shrink wrapping their kits at source, although this has a double-edged advantage. You know that the model is the same as when it left the factory, but you can't examine it in the shop if you want to and, if anything should be missing, this will not become apparent until you reach home. However, all companies and distributors run a spare parts service so, even if a part is missing or damaged, it will not necessarily mean abandoning the whole kit to the spare parts bin.

THE COMPANIES

The boom period for plastic kit production was probably during the 60s and it was at this time that most kit companies flourished. However, the plastics industry is heavily dependent on the oil industry and, although in the 60s everything seemed fine, the 70s brought the oil crisis and the price of raw materials rocketed. This drastically affected the model companies and some went under, never to return. Such famous names as Aurora were lost along with Frog, though their tooling went respectively to Monogram and the Soviet company Novo, with some Frog tooling going to Revell.

This was not to be the end of the model company's troubles though, because general business problems seemed to hit virtually every name in the modelling world in the mid to late 70s. Famous names nearly lost were Airfix, Revell and Matchbox and, through their association with parent companies, AMT and MPC as well. Some appear to have ridden the storm. Lindberg, one of the oldest original companies, continued in a relatively small way, which perhaps was the key to its survival. The Italian companies, Italeri and ESCI also survived, along with French Heller. But by now the Japanese had a strong grip on the modelling industry with names such as Tamiya and Hasegawa becoming almost as much household names as Revell and Airfix.

By the 80s, the industry had sorted itself out and had in fact banded together in an effort to survive, with previous rivals becoming partners. At this moment in time the situation has settled as follows. In Britain, Humbrol owns both Airfix and Heller, with moulding being done in France. Matchbox continues, though it has lost its original take-over of the AMT name. AMT has reverted back to American ownership and forms part of the kit side of ERTL alongside its one-time opponent, MPC. Most recently, ERTL acquired the ESCI line and continues the name in Europe, although uses the AMT logo in America.

The two other big names on the American kit scene, Revell and Monogram, are now jointly owned under the Odyssey Partners holding company. Revell moved from its long-time base in Venice, California, where it had begun as Precision Specialities in the Gowland and Gowland era, and moved to Des Plaines, Illinois, a city on the outskirts of Chicago and very near to its new stable mate Monogram in Morton Grove. Revell Europe still runs as a more or less separate company with its own catalogue, the only 'name' to do so, and is now run from the German base rather than the original British, the changeover having been completed when Revell was temporarily French-owned as part of the Joustra group.

Still in America, Testors, the larger of the two model paint and accessory manufacturers, the other being Pactra, took over a number of the tooling from older names such as Hawk and IMC and continues to reissue some of the kits. It also has a tie-in with Italeri in Italy and Fujimi in Japan. Some old manufacturers tooling also still exists, with, as mentioned, Aurora's moulds going to Monogram and another original name, Renwall, being taken over by Revell in the mid-70s. Only two of the early names, Lindberg and Jo-Han, survive by themselves, although even Lindberg acquired some other tooling, mainly from Pyro and its later reincarnation Life-Like.

In the rest of continental Europe some other names continue but, invariably with specialist subjects, usually railways, with Faller and Heljan being the best known, Faller having long ago abandoned its famous range of 1:100 scale aircraft and missile subjects. In Japan things are probably less certain and, although names such as Tamiya and Hasegawa have been joined by Gunze Sangyo and Fujimi amongst the big league, other smaller names still around are Nichimo, Arii and Doyusha. We've also seen in the 80s the growth of other far eastern industries at the expense of Japan, from Taiwan, Korea and Hong Kong, usually with a tie-in with other 'western' companies where a change of name sometimes takes place.

These are full scale companies producing models by conventional injection processes, but, since the oil crisis in the

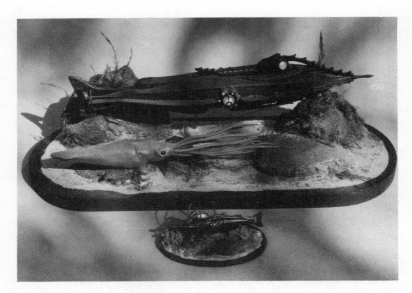

The 80s has seen a rapid growth in the 'cottage' or 'garage' industries. Science fiction has been a natural for this side of the hobby, typified by these two Comet Miniatures examples of Jules Verne's Nautilus submarine. The larger is built up from vacformed and white metal parts, while the smaller is totally white metal. In both cases the bases and squids are scratchbuilt.

70s, another aspect of the hobby has developed, that of the 'cottage' or 'garage' industries. These are small businesses, invariably one-man operated, and many are part-time industries producing short runs of specialist parts for the dedicated modeller. Most are concerned with the aircraft side of the hobby, as it does account for half of the products in general, and the garage industries seem content to produce items that the established kit companies would not touch. The methods used to produce these garage kits involve virtually every moulding method, except injection, it being the most costly by far, and great efforts have been made developing other moulding methods that are less expensive for producing finished results, though are more labour intensive.

Most of the garage kits have utilised the vacuum formed method in their manufacture. The quality of the result can, in fact, be extremely detailed, although this depends on the original mould and which type of vacforming has been used. Vacforming, however, is unsuitable for producing delicate parts, such as undercarriage legs, so other methods have been adapted, particularly white metal. This is a low melting alloy, used mainly for wargaming-type figures. Because of its low melting point it can be used in moulds that would not tolerate higher temperatures, so can be made from tough rubber or resins.

Resin itself is a material being used more often for these limited production kits, and here virtually all the parts—large and small—can be made of this material. It is, however, brittle and needs care in handling, cleaning up and assembly. All of which only proves the versatility of the injection moulded styrene parts, which perform all these tasks with ease.

More recently, new techniques have allowed for short runs of kits to be made using the injection process, but into a mould far less substantial than the hard steel tooling usually used. This has led to specialist companies making complete aircraft kits that match roughly the layout of the conventional moulded products, though more cleaning up is required around the parts. Depending on the original mould and the way it is used, runs up to 1,000 can be obtained, although this is nothing when it is realised that steel tooling can still be used after producing several million kits.

The limited run 'garage' techniques are also suitable for

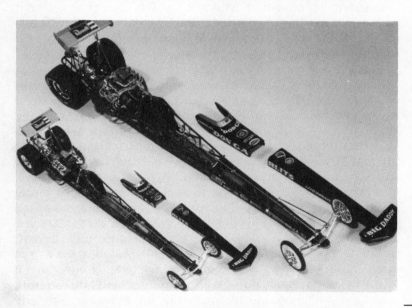

Revell's 1:16 and 1:25 scale versions of Don Garlits rear-engined dragster.

other subjects besides aircraft, and parts for AFVs were next to be produced. Then came a growth in the car and truck modelling area, producing bodies and accessories to go with existing chassis, while the science fiction modeller also benefited from the growth in this side of the hobby.

SCALES

This is a subject guaranteed to get most modellers expounding their views, particularly when it comes to the various merits of one size of model when compared to another, or why a manufacturer has ignored this scale at the expense of an alternative. The exact history as to why certain scales were adopted is also guaranteed to cause an equally heated discussion, although it is probably safe to say that the most popular scale 1:72, for the most common subject, aircraft, came about as a direct spin-off from the earlier recognition models, also of the same size. Exactly why the size was originally chosen is not certain but one possibility is that it is a convenient scale that can show a fighter against a bomber without either being too large or too small. It is also a standard linear reduction using imperial measurements and here it is interesting to note that choice of scales seems to be split between those that are related to the imperial system and those related to the metric, though even here it is not as logical as it would initially appear.

Staying with the imperial sizes, the choice of 1:144 scale for airliners, initially from Airfix, was logical as it was exactly half of 1:72 scale. This was also followed through for their series of space launchers, Saturn 5 and the like, and was duplicated by Monogram. For the larger scales, these again are simple engineering reductions from full size, 1:48 being ¼ in. to the foot; 1 : 32 = ⅜ in. – foot and 1 : 24 = ½ in. – foot. Because the kit industry was born in America and Britain, the use of imperial reduction scales was in fact logical, and when continental Europe began manufacturing, it was also logical that they used the metric reduction, Faller for example, settling for 1 : 100 scale and Heller for 1:125, 1:100 and 1:50 scales for their aircraft subjects. However, 1:72 scale was firmly established as the premier aircraft scale and, in more recent years, Heller moved over to adopt this non-metric size, for military aircraft, although retaining the metric 1:125 for airliners. Similarly Japan, ostensibly metric, wanted to cater for both ranges and so aircraft in particular can be found in 1:100 scale, Tamiya's military aircraft; 1:200, Hasegawa's airliners, as well as 1:72, 1:48 and 1:32 scales.

With car models, the first were produced in 1:32 scale from Gowland and Gowland and, although this arguably is a standard $\frac{3}{8}$ in. – foot reduction, it actually came about more by chance as a simple halving of a scale the company was using for their toy-like car models. This happened to be 1 : 16 scale, (which is $\frac{3}{4}$ in. – foot), hence 1 : 32 scale. The larger models began as 1:25 scale from AMT, Jo-Han and Revell. The first two were engaged in making promotional models (promos) for the full-scale car companies, and the scale was dictated by the latter as a 2½ reduction from their 1:10 scale plans, hence we ended up with what could be termed a 'metric' reduction in a very 'imperial' country. Revell, although not actively engaged in promotional models, were working with AMT, so adopted the same scale.

When Aurora began model car production, they too adopted 1:25 scale as did IMC. However, Monogram who had no 'promotional' ties, used the perhaps more logical imperial ½ in. – foot, i.e. 1 : 24 scale, as did Lindberg and Pyro for the few kits they made in the larger scale. When European countries and Japan started to produce larger scale car kits, they too opted for the imperial 1 : 24 scale which is still used by Italeri, ESCI, Tamiya, Fujimi, Hasegawa, Gunze Sangyo and others. When Airfix made larger scaled car kits they used 1:24 scale, although most were in 1:32 scale as a direct response to the Gowland and Gowland and Revell originals. Matchbox followed suit when they began kit production as against diecasts, and in previous years this scale was the main output from Aurora, Pyro and Lindberg.

However, it's safe to say that no kit company will start a new series of models without regard to scale these days, and this even applies to the largest subject usually kitted – ships. Here the choice of scales is at its widest and, although a number of the earliest Revell warships were built to fit the box, when Airfix began their modern warship series, they adopted a constant scale of 1:600. These days 1:700 scale appears to be the accepted scale for such craft, although deviations, such as 1:720 scale, and halving to 1:350 scale appear common, and Heller use 1:400 scale. With galleon models, scales are nothing like as clear and those examples from Airfix, Heller and Revell are still built to an overall size rather than a constant scale.

1 BUILDING INJECTION KITS

GEOFF PRENTICE

The most important question to ask yourself when you decide to build a kit is 'why?'. Not 'why not do something useful like homework or house decorating instead?', but 'why do I want to build this kit?' That may sound absurd, but failure to identify your purpose at an early stage is probably the main reason for all the incomplete models in the world. There are no bad reasons for kit building: you may have a special interest in the subject; you may be interested in the challenge of building a particular kit; you may have a competition in mind; you might want to build a collection; or you may simply want to while away a few hours in a constructive fashion. Knowing your purpose will help you gain satisfaction from the project, whatever your standard, and will enhance your prospects of succeeding.

Kit selection
Having established your motivation, the next stage is to select your kit. Many of the most popular subjects are available in a variety of forms and the choice you make now will certainly determine the nature of the job ahead. First you should check to make sure that the kit fills your particular needs. Is it the right mark? Does it offer the markings you require? Has it the appropriate weapons or accessories for the model you have in mind? Assuming you are still left with a choice, then you must seek the best kit for your purpose.

Price is not always an infallible guide, neither is the beguiling 'New' label on the box. There are some very good cheap kits and some terribly expensive ones. Manufacturers are not above putting a 'New' flash on the box of a 20 year old kit simply because they have changed the decals or have done some minor modifications to the mould. Most model shop proprietors will be pleased to advise you and to let you look inside the box. Failing that, look for reviews or articles in the modelling press or, probably best of all, ask other modellers for their views.

Preparation

Once you have chosen your kit, spend a little time getting to know it. First look through the instructions to get an idea of how the thing fits together. In some cases the sequence of certain operations is critical and it is important to know what it is. Remember, however, that kit instruction sheets are often designed with simplicity and economy of production in mind. Therefore, they may advise you to do certain jobs at a particular stage, simply because it saves putting an extra drawing on the sheet. This is more annoying than critical but, if you stick a small or delicate part on the outer surface of the model at stage one, then you can rely on having to replace or repair it two or three times before the model is finished. Get a clear picture of how the main construction is undertaken and also decide what smaller parts can be left to a later stage in order to avoid damaging them.

While checking the instructions it is a good idea to identify the various parts on the sprues (the framework on which the parts are moulded) as you go. It is also the time to check for damage or loose items. Carry out any necessary repairs now and put all the stray parts in a safe place. It may be some time before you need the particular parts; remembering that you saw them when you opened the box is scant consolation if they are not there when you need them later.

Cutting out

The point at which the sprue joins the part is called the 'gate' and the temptation is to break the parts away from the

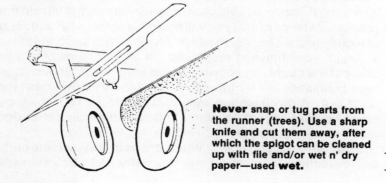

Never snap or tug parts from the runner (trees). Use a sharp knife and cut them away, after which the spigot can be cleaned up with file and/or wet n' dry paper—used **wet.**

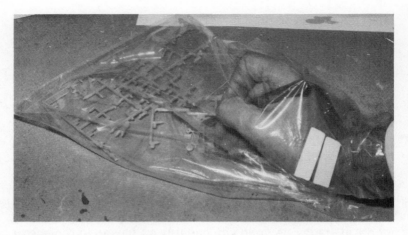

You will never see a small part vanish into the carpet if you cut off the sprue inside a plastic bag.

framework by snapping the thin gate plastic. Don't. You stand a very good chance of leaving a scar on large parts and damaging small ones. Always cut through the gate with a sharp knife or nail cutters, then trim the excess material from the part very carefully with your knife. When releasing small items in this way (a job that should never be done until they are needed) they are inclined to fly about the room and get lost. There are two ways of preventing this: either make sure you hold the part, not the sprue or put the sprue in a plastic bag so that if the part does go ballistic it is trapped by the bag.

Test fitting

Having released the major components, test fit them in the way indicated by the instructions. The very best kits will fit perfectly with almost imperceptible seam lines. Sadly, many kits do not reach that standard and you will find misalignment of parts and unsightly gaps. The way in which you deal with these will make or break your finished model, so it's as well to eliminate as many of the causes as possible at this early stage. Some edges have blemishes left by the gates, or by the pins that push the parts out of the injection mould. These may be erased by careful paring with a modelling knife or by sanding the edge with fine abrasive paper.

Often the pegs and holes intended to help you align the parts are misaligned themselves and make the parts difficult to fit

Cleaning up mould lines and improving the shape of intakes and cowling lips can make a major difference to the appearance of the model. Here the cowlings of a Matchbox Wellington are being refined.

together or make them fit improperly. If this is the case, double check to make sure you haven't made a mistake for which you are blaming the kit, then trim the pegs off with your knife. Tab slots, like those at wing or tailplane roots, may be obstructed or too tight. Once again, double check them and adjust with a knife.

Washing

By now you should be fairly familiar with the kit and be anxious to get on with the assembly, but first wash the kit in water with a

Below, washing all kit parts in mild detergent and warm water is an essential preparatory chore prior to assembly. Cleansing removes mould release oil and aids adhesion of both cement and paint. After drying, handle the parts as little as possible with your hands—tweezers and/or tissues are preferable.

little washing-up liquid and allow it to dry (don't use hot water or apply heat to speed drying because heat distorts plastic). This removes any traces of the fluid used to help release the parts from the mould and prevents it hindering adhesion or spoiling the paintwork later on. Note: opinions vary about the need for this, and many fine modellers never bother. The use of release agent is not universal among manufacturers and problems of this kind are few and far between. On the other hand, it takes only a few moments to wash a kit so I commend the practice on the grounds that it is better to be safe than sorry.

Adhesives

Since 99% of kit assembly is done with adhesive of one kind or another, now seems a good time for a short digression on the subject of 'glue'. The misuse of 'glue' causes more problems to the modeller than any other medium. Generally the difficulties arise because too much is used at one time or because it gets in the wrong place.

Essentially 'glues' come in two forms: the ones that soften the surfaces of the parts and allow them to weld together, and those that adhere to the surface without attacking it and form a layer between the mating surfaces which bonds them. Chemists will probably protest that this is gross oversimplification but, for practical purposes, that is all *we* really need to consider.

Of the two types, the first is by far the more important and potentially destructive. It comes in many forms and the experienced modeller will adopt two or three to be used for various purposes. The most common is tube cement. At one time this was the only glue available and it is still the substance most often pressed on the new modeller. It is very strong when set and has its uses for high stress joints. It tends to set slowly and forms strings when handled in a part-cured state. It is the most prone to excessive application since it is very difficult to apply in small quantities. I don't deny its value in certain circumstances, but my advice to any beginner is not to use it.

In recent years liquid cement has become widely available in a variety of forms and this should be your staple 'glue'. It comes in jars and bottles and varies considerably in strength depending on the blend of solvents employed. All of the proprietary brands are satisfactory and you should experiment to find the ones that suit you best. Personally, I use a mild liquid cement for general purpose work and keep one of the stronger liquid welds for tricky areas and special jobs where a strong bond with the absolute minimum of glue is necessary, but it is very much a matter of taste.

Many of the liquids come supplied with little brushes, though these are of only limited value. They can be used to pre-coat wide areas like trailing edges to help them get an initial bond, but the liquids are far more effective when applied to a closed joint with a very fine brush, syringe or, my preference, a fine mapping pen. Simply hold the joint together and apply the loaded pen to the seam line. Capillary action will take the liquid some distance along the joint which will bond in a few moments. Long joints can be worked around a few inches at a time squeezing each section gently as it cures to ensure a good bond and to help fill the seam. This technique takes a little practice but it is well worth the trouble. It is particularly valuable when pulling together warped or distorted parts.

If you do happen to put on too much, or spill some in the wrong place, don't try to wipe it off. Let it dry then tackle the damage. Paint has a surprising capacity to protect plastic from the effects of liquid and tube cements so be sure to avoid leaving it on any surfaces you are hoping to bond.

There is an unwritten law of modelling that 'the glue runs out when the hobby shop is shut'! This is particularly true of the liquids and, the stronger and more volatile they are, the quicker they evaporate. Get into the habit of replacing the lid every time

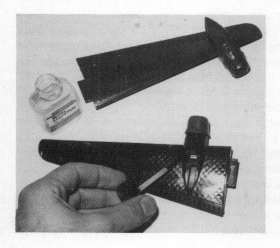

Liquid glue can be flowed into joints after the parts have been positioned. This reduces the likelihood of damage to surrounding areas.

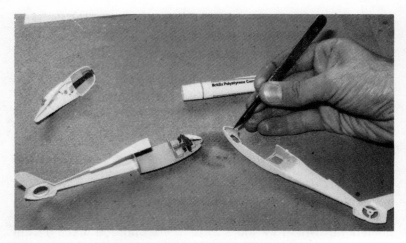

**Scrape paint from all joint areas before trying to join them!
The tube glue is not generally recommended however.**

you have finished using it. Stability is also important when it comes to glue bottles and, as many manufacturers overlook the fact, you must make amends. I tend to decant all liquids into spare Humbrol bottles; they are short and square and very stable. If you can't get these, then try sticking a square of card to the base of unstable bottles or fix them to your building board with a blob of Blu-Tack.

Now let's look at the other glues that will feature in your modelling box. First in importance are the 'super glues' or cyanoacrylates. These are very fast acting and give you very little time to align parts with no second chances. They have considerable tensile strength, but very little shear strength. In other words, they are hard to pull apart but will fail quite easily if lateral force is applied. That makes them a poor bet for joining fuselage halves which may flex with handling, but very good for fixing small parts into holes.

They will bond dissimilar materials, so are invaluable for fixing the metal parts that come with modern kits, or are purchased as 'extras'. They will also take on paint so, if you find you must stick something to a painted surface, then this is your method. Beware; they are also capable of pulling paint off plastic so don't use it on parts that will be stressed later.

Aside from the obvious uses, like fixing undercarriage doors and the like, my favourite use for cyano is to 'spot weld' wing joints where I need to set up a particular dihedral angle. Normal cements take too long to cure, so it is necessary to support the wing in some form of simple jig while it dries to prevent sagging. A couple of spots of cyano will enable you to set the angle permanently in seconds (use the thicker 'gap filling' variety which cures slightly slower); once it has set, reinforce the joint by running in liquid glue to weld it.

Since cyano dries clear, it appeared at first to be the ideal way of fixing clear parts. Unfortunately it gives off fumes which fog clear plastic with a fine white powder. If you can get to both sides of the clear part after it has set then no problem, because you can clean off the powder with a Q-tip. If you cannot, and that is generally the case with canopies, then don't use cyano.

White glue, PVA or woodworker's glue, are all pretty much the same. They are water-based glues that don't attack the plastic, but which will give a soft bond between plastic parts. Unlike all other adhesives, any excess can be wiped away with a damp cloth or Q-tip and you can re-open any joint they make without damage to the parts. They dry clear and will fill small gaps. They are not strong enough for main joints but are much favoured for fixing clear parts. When dry, they have a rubbery consistency and are slightly flexible. This gives them a valuable 'shock-absorbing' quality which makes them ideal for fixing models to bases.

This can only be a short appraisal of the numerous 'glues' available. In a meeting of modellers you may hear many others mentioned and their virtues extolled. Many have merits, but all have drawbacks. The average modeller's bench holds a number of products which have been tried but relegated to obscurity. Never be afraid to try new ideas, but always remember to read the instructions and, in particular, the safety advice carefully. Cyano bonds skin instantly and has toxic fumes. Solvent based liquids can give you a nasty headache, or worse, and many have adverse effects on your skin after prolonged contact. Treated with respect, they will work hard and safely for you, so take care.

Construction

After that serious note let's get back to the fun and look at the main construction process. Assuming that you have followed the advice above, and have familiarised yourself with the kit and rectified any obvious fitting difficulties, there should be few problems at this stage. There are, however, one or two points worth noting as you proceed. Many kits are designed in such a way that some areas of the interior can be seen through canopies, windows or other apertures. If these are areas of detail then you will have painted them before assembly but, quite often, they are simply the interior of the moulded shell. The instructions will probably tell you to paint an indeterminate area before assembly, but it is all too easy to paint too little and end up with an unsightly patch of coloured plastic that can be seen and which is beyond the reach of any paintbrush. The remedy is simple. Paint the complete interior of any part that just might be seen before you seal it forever; wasted paint is preferable to bare plastic any time.

Another similar problem is that of 'see-through'. This is most common in elderly kits of jet aircraft but it can occur in any kit with an oversimplified interior structure. In its simplest form it results in a model with a totally empty interior and a clear view from intake to jet pipe, but it can occur in many other models where an aperture gives visual access to an excessive area of the interior. The cure is simple with a little foresight. Crude plastic card blanking plates can be installed some way behind the hole to cut out the view while not depriving the hole of depth. As your technique advances, you may well want to add detail to the interior, but in the early stages a simple disc or rough bulkhead will suffice.

Aircraft kits nearly always start with cockpit interiors which are built and painted to taste and fixed in one fuselage half.

Adding weight, in this case a screw pressed into some Plasticine in the nose of a Lightning kit.

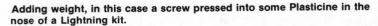

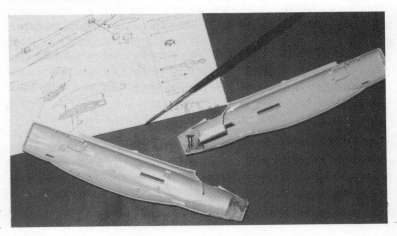

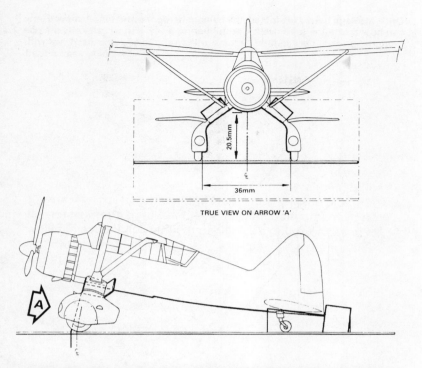

TRUE VIEW ON ARROW 'A'

Complex jigs can be made for specific purposes from card or stiff paper. These drawings were prepared for a Matchbox Lysander which had undergone major corrective surgery to its main undercarriage.

Before you glue them in place do a dry run with the other fuselage half to check that they are not going to cause difficulties when it is put in place. A little trimming now can save problems later. It is also important to make sure that any part fixed to one half of a shell is properly aligned. Cockpit interiors, in particular, have a habit of sagging while they are drying and either won't line up with the location points in the other fuselage half or sit at a drunken angle. Either hold them square until they dry, or use an adhesive with a slower drying time. Dry fit the other fuselage half in place and secure it with tape or rubber bands to act as a jig while the interior parts set.

Haste is the greatest enemy to a good model. Work slowly and methodically and give all major parts a reasonable time to dry before proceeding. Many models are spoiled by poor alignment which often goes unnoticed until the model is completed. There are few more discouraging experiences than showing off your latest creation to someone who points out

Once fuselage halves are joined, the cement hardened and tape removed, one can now tackle the joint itself. Careful paring away with a craft knife may be required prior to careful final sanding with 'wet n' dry' paper used wet with some soap added.

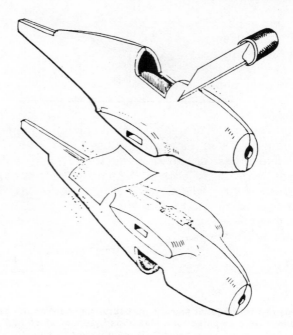

that the tail-fin leans or that one wing droops. Always check your model from front and rear during construction and, if you have any doubts about the strength of something you have just glued in place, prop it up in a simple jig while it hardens. Jigs don't have to be complex: piles of coins or paint tins are ideal supports for wings and tails and, if someone in the family has some Lego bricks, quite complicated supports can be custom-made in a few moments! Undercarriages and wheels can also be saved from the 'leans' in this way. Set them at the correct angles then support the model while they harden with the wheels just touching a flat surface.

Seams
No matter how good a kit is and how careful your construction, you are bound to have some seam lines which require attention. Hopefully, the majority will have been rendered invisible by virtue of the tiny bead of plastic that you squeezed

out of the joint while gluing. Then all you need do is to trim that off with a knife or very fine (600 grade) wet and dry paper. Elsewhere, one edge of a joint will be higher than the other, and perhaps, there will even be the odd gap.

Detecting the irregularities is critical because otherwise the final paint job will show them up. I run my fingernail across all joints and treat any area where I feel a slight 'catch'. Another effective method is to sand all joints very lightly with worn 600 paper. The neat joins will sand evenly but low spots will not be touched and will remain shiny in contrast to the duller sanded area. Where this occurs you must decide whether further sanding will solve the problem without corrupting the outline of the model or, if it is necessary, to use filler.

Fillers, like glues, come in many forms each with their advantages and disadvantages. Some attack the plastic surface and key themselves to it, others do not. Some require sealing before painting, some do not; all shrink to some degree as they dry but some will go on shrinking for months, or even years, after application. It is very much a matter of personal preference and, like glues, you will probably find that you like to keep two or three varieties to hand for different purposes. My personal preference for general purposes is Milliput, a two-part material that can be used as mixed for gap filling or diluted with water for seams. It has one major advantage in that it can be worked with a wet finger or Q-tip even when part-set and that reduces sanding time and consequent damage to surface detail considerably.

The essence of all filling is to keep the thickness of filler to a minimum. There is little point in smothering a minor seam defect in filler only to sand 99% of it off again. It is far better to reduce the defect as much as possible by sanding and then use the filler as the finishing touch. I apply Milliput wet with a blunt scalpel blade working along the line of the joint. This enables the blade to ride on the high side of the joint and to deposit the filler on the low side. The method is rather like buttering bread with the sharp edge of the knife trailing. I allow Milliput to dry slightly and then reduce any excess thickness with a wet finger. Some people can eliminate the need for further sanding entirely in this way. However, I prefer to finish the job with progressively finer grades of wet and dry until the joint is invisible.

When sanding seam lines, it is all too easy to get carried away and to make the joint vanish at the expense of the shape of the

Vacform techniques come in useful when dealing with some short-run injection kits. Here the fuselage halves are being cleaned up to improve the joint line.

part. The damage is not always apparent until after painting when square wing leading edges, or unrealistic flat areas on curved fuselages, become glaringly obvious. Much of this problem can be avoided by sanding to and fro across the joint thus allowing the paper to follow the curves of the part. Do this by holding the strip of paper at the ends and avoid applying direct pressure to the seam line. There is a simple little tool called a Flexi-File that makes this easier.

It is also possible to make a sanding block which conforms to any particular curve. I have an aged block of soft balsa wood with a host of different curves both concave and convex on its worn surfaces. To create these I hold a piece of sandpaper tightly around the model in the area to be sanded with the abrasive side outwards. I rub the block on that until a rough impression of the surface is shaped. I then reverse the paper and hold it over the shaped area of the block and commence sanding. As a method it's cheap and unsophisticated, but it works.

The final check on seam work comes at quite a late stage in the project. Before painting, prime the model with a coat of pale grey paint (I use aerosol auto-primer but check its compatibility with the plastic on a piece of scrap first). This will show up any poor seams or other defects at a stage when you can rectify them without destroying your finished paintwork. The answer to seams in simple terms is care, attention to detail, and a stubborn determination not to settle for second best. There is no seam that cannot be eliminated and, as your technique progresses, you will find that the majority succumb quite easily.

Spraying with aerosol auto-primer.

Clear parts

Often the bane of the novice modeller, clear parts demand just a little more care. The main problem is that all the conventional plastic glues cloud them on contact so you have to avoid getting any of those glues anywhere that you need to be crystal clear. The easy way out is not to use a solvent-based glue but one of the PVA family. These give you a second, third or fourth chance if you need them, and will never harm the canopy, however badly you treat it. Excess can be removed with a little water and the glue helps to seal the gaps.

Seams around clear parts are one of the commonest faults, persisting even on the work of quite experienced modellers. They indicate a reluctance to fill, or sand around the delicate parts, and are totally unnecessary. Once the transparent areas are properly masked you can do anything to the rest of them and, even if you do get a blemish on the outside, it can be polished away.

There are a number of paint-on masking mediums available and, though I personally loathe them, they work well for people who don't mind ruining paintbrushes! Without exception, they all lack the protective qualities of masking tape and this is what you must use if you plan to do any filling. Coat the clear parts in a layer of top-quality tape, 3M invisible tape or similar, and then cut away the tape over the frame-lines or other solid areas. With the clear parts protected you can then use your filler with impunity provided you don't get the work too wet and cause the tape to lift. You can sand as necessary to blend the canopy, or whatever, into the surrounding structure. Once removed, the tape will expose undamaged clear panels.

Sometimes the shape of the clear part is so wrong that you will have to reshape it to an extent that requires you to sand the clear areas. Treat this like any other sanding job and finish it off with your finest grades of paper to eliminate all but the finest scratches, then repolish. Denim is a good polishing cloth for fine scratches and a brisk rub on your jeans will work wonders. If further assistance is needed, then there are a number of mediums that work well. Toothpaste or powder does work, though I find it tedious and rather messy. The various abrasive polishes sold for removing minor blemishes from car paint-work are better and a variety of metal polishes work well, as do the various liquids sold as model canopy polishes. The thing to remember when experimenting is that not all clear plastic parts are the same material and it is imperative to test any of the more active polishes on a piece of sprue first. I had one favourite car polish that worked wonders on all canopies except Monogram's which crazed on contact!

Over-thick clear parts are quite common in commercial kits and can detract from the finished model. Vacforming replacements is one solution if you have the equipment, there are also some excellent commercial vacform parts available for many popular subjects. If neither option is available to you then you can improve the situation by painting the edges of the clear parts flat black, or dark grey, before fixing them in place. This reduces the internal reflections within the parts and makes them appear thinner. It is a good idea to treat all clear parts this way as a precaution. The final polish can be added to clear parts with an overspray of clear wax polish. Klear, or its US equivalent Future, are ideal as either will impart a sheen and hide any minor imperfections.

Tools

Every modeller has tools that he cannot live without and those that he thought would solve all his problems but which he finds he hardly ever uses. Discounting items like pliers and clothes pegs which most households have about anyway, here is my list of absolute essentials:

1 A good modelling knife and a selection of blades. This is as vital to the modeller as a pen is to a writer and it pays to get the best. In my opinion that means the long-handled Swan-Morton scalpel, if it's good enough for surgeons, then it's good enough for you; they also make a short handled version which lacks the perfect balance of its brother but is handy for heavier work. If you can't get either then opt for the No.11 Exacto knife.

2 Tweezers – the answer to all those folk who ask how you can do fine work with fat fingers. The most important pair(s) are the ones with fine points available from specialist tool suppliers or surgical equipment agents. Get a pair that feel comfortable and that has points that won't cross over. There are hosts of other kinds about that come in useful for certain jobs but none are essential; if you are looking to expand your basic toolset then the type that are sprung closed and open when you squeeze them are handy.

3 Small files, in a variety of shapes, are invaluable for cleaning out apertures or making parts fit location holes. Working with plastic you won't need the best metalworker's tools, but don't buy the cheapest either. Plastic tends to clog files so invest in a cheap wire suede brush from the shoe shop to clean them out.

4 Abrasive paper in a variety of grades is an absolute must. Again go for a decent quality—your local DIY car shop should stock wet and dry paper in the grades you need (220–600 or finer if you can get it). Save worn out 600 grade for extra fine work and, if you are short of a fine grade at any time, remember that you can reduce coarser papers somewhat by rubbing them together.

Modifications and improvements

This very complex subject justifies its own chapter (see elsewhere in this book) so great is the potential offered by even the most basic of kits to someone with skill and imagination. At the beginning of this chapter I said that defining your motives was important. That is so because it will determine your requirements for personal satisfaction. You may well decide that assembling kits as they are designed is all you want to do and will spend a happy and rewarding modelling career doing just that. On the other hand, you may tire of basic kit building and want to make your model different from the rest. You will probably start with basic improvements, like flattening tyres to indicate weight, opening canopies and hatches or cutting out flying controls and lowering flaps.

Next comes cross-kitting to change the variant to one not otherwise available, or simply to combine the best features of

Never neglect old kits as they can give you a lot of fun. This is not the modern Italeri AC-119K but a 1950s Aurora kit. Milliput formed the nose, the jet pods and the master for the replacement vacform canopy.

One of the most effective ways of making a naval aircraft model look different is to fold its wings.

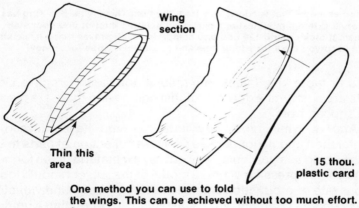

Wing section

Thin this area

15 thou. plastic card

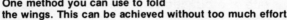

One method you can use to fold the wings. This can be achieved without too much effort.

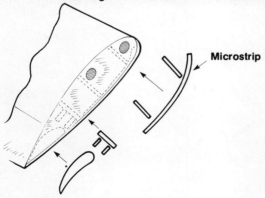

Microstrip

Another model that is a long way from the box. This Fujimi Sea King has over 40 external modifications plus a scratchbuilt interior and door step detail. It took around 120 hours to complete which proves that a basic kit can keep you busy for a long time and is excellent value for money!

two or more kits. Injection moulded and vacform conversion kits are a natural extension of this course and there are plenty to choose from.

After a while, you may find that you have crossed a watershed and no longer see a kit as a collection of parts to be assembled in a particular way but as raw material to be formed into your impression of how a model of the subject should look. Your rate of production will fall alarmingly but, if individuality has become your aim, your satisfaction in producing a unique replica should increase in proportion.

2   AIRCRAFT CONVERSIONS ON A BUDGET

ROBERT HUMPHREYS

Two of my favourite aircraft are the Supermarine Spitfire and the Hawker Hurricane, and I have several examples of both types in my collection. One of my long term modelling ambitions is to build a model of every variant of both types. In the case of the Hurricane this is not too difficult to achieve, but for the Spitfire (and Seafire) it is a mammoth task! To confine oneself to the building of one or two types only would be detrimental to the project, finally resulting in a lowering of standards, and a decline in the pleasure to be obtained from the project.

Consequently, I try to work these two projects into other projects which I have an interest in. In other words, I have several on-going projects, each one complementing and supplementing the other. The chart below, by no means definitive, may help to clarify the point I am trying to make.

By following such themes, or even other projects representing events from other periods in time, the modeller can quite happily add to his collection by building his models straight from the box. However, a time may come when a particular variant is needed for the collection which is not commercially

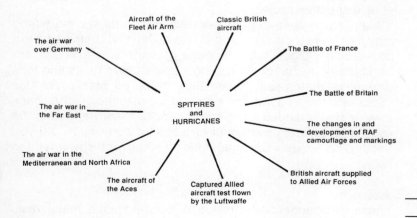

Aircraft of the Fleet Air Arm

Classic British aircraft

The air war over Germany

The Battle of France

The air war in the Far East

SPITFIRES and HURRICANES

The Battle of Britain

The changes in and development of RAF camouflage and markings

The air war in the Mediterranean and North Africa

British aircraft supplied to Allied Air Forces

The aircraft of the Aces

Captured Allied aircraft test flown by the Luftwaffe

available. If the modeller is anxious enough to acquire such a variant the only course of action open to him may be to produce it himself. This is known as a conversion, the difficulty of which depends on the amount of work which needs to be done.

Of course, the simplest of all conversions is changing the colour scheme and/or markings of the models. This in itself can produce some interesting and eye-catching finishes. Other conversions may call for the use of items from the spares box, the purchase of accessories from model shops, the use of plastic card and various fillers plus different types of adhesive. In fact, specialist tools may be needed for the task, as well as specific decals for the finish of the model. In addition to this, the modeller will have to consult plenty of references *before* he even considers taking his knife to the plastic. But first of all let's take a closer look at these items to see what use they are to us.

The spares box

This is a collection of various parts which are kept for possible use in the future. Their origins may be many and varied. Several kits nowadays provide alternative parts to enable the kit to be finished as one of many possible variants. Don't throw away these 'left-overs'. Instead, keep them, as they may be needed at a future date.

Likewise, a completed model which has been damaged, or is no longer to be displayed, should never be thrown away. Deposit it in the spares box, and at some time in the future, you may be able to cannibalise it for a project. In time, perhaps you can get together with other modellers for a 'spares swap' for your respective projects.

Many items seemingly unconnected with plastic modelling may also have their uses, and may one day find their way into a conversion. Cigar tube holders of various diameters are particularly useful for simulating jet pipes. Biro tubes and tops also have their uses. Those little coloured plastic cocktail sticks are very useful for simulating navigation lights once they've been sanded to shape. In short, most things can be used as they are, or adapted for use in a conversion. All you need to do is use your imagination and never throw anything away!

Accessories

These are commercially produced items in plastic, metal, resin or acetate and are available from model shops, mail order companies or cottage industries. They range in scale, and practically all items you could conceivably want are available, from WW1 engines and machine-guns to jet aircraft access ladders and runway matting. These accessories can save the modeller a lot of time and effort.

Plastic card and Acetate

Plastic card is a very useful product. Basically a sheet of plastic, these range in thickness and can be cut and shaped according to the needs of the modeller. Again, your imagination is practically the only limit here.

Acetate film is clear plastic, and very useful for such items as canopies etc. A good source of acetate film is the plastic bubble container on children's toys so, again, never throw anything away.

Fillers and body putty

A wide range of fillers and body putty is available, so it is simply a matter of finding the one that suits you best. These have a range of uses from filling joint lines to being used to alter the outline of the model.

Adhesives

Again, a wide range is available. However, I find that liquid and tube polystyrene cements are adequate for most conversions with the occasional use of super glue for metal items, and PVA adhesive for fixing canopies in place. PVA has the added advantage of drying clear, and may also be used to fill hairline joints.

Abrasives and files

Years ago, I bought a wallet of six files of various sizes and shapes from a market stall and I find these very useful for major sanding work. Finer sanding can be done with various grades of wet 'n' dry paper, available from motor accessory shops or hardware stores.

Knives and razor saws

Here again we have many types to choose from. The craft knife which I have used for many years is a Swann-Morton, which has three different styles of blades contained within the handle.

Both the knife itself and replacement blades are widely available and inexpensive.

Razor saws are fine toothed blades which are used when major surgery needs to be performed on a kit during a conversion. Several types are available, so it's a matter of finding what you feel comfortable with.

Tweezers

This little instrument is ideal for placing small items when fingers are too clumsy to do the job. Again, several styles are widely available, so go for what you can afford.

Paint and brushes

You should always buy the best quality brushes you can afford. Paints should be mixed thoroughly before each application and the lid replaced on each tinlet immediately after you have finished with it. If you have cause to mix various colours to produce a particular shade or hue, remember to keep a note of the colours used, and in what ratio, as it may come in useful again.

The decal bank

This is a store of decals which are left over items from those supplied in various kits, and/or which have been purchased from specialist manufacturers. A vast range of decals is available, so there is very little excuse for not being able to finish your latest masterpiece in its proper markings. Even though some of these decal sheets are a bit on the expensive side, several models can usually be finished from each, so in effect you get very good value for money. Never throw a decal sheet, or even part of one, away as it may be used, or modified for use, in the future. Keep your decals clean and dry in a tin or box, filed perhaps according to type, nationality or era.

Now let's model!

Up to now, all this is mere theory, so let's try putting it into practice. The main aim of the following conversions is to attempt to illustrate some of the different techniques and materials which can be used. Consequently, no attempt has been made to diversify the subject matter, and each conversion is based on inexpensive and easily obtainable kits of the Spitfire. The degree of difficulty of each conversion varies, but each procedure used can be adapted and/or applied to any type which the modeller chooses to build.

CONVERSION 1

Subject – Spitfire Mk. 1a, K9942, as preserved at the RAF Museum, Hendon. This is the oldest preserved Spitfire, coming from the initial production batch. It is also reputed to have been flown by Flt. Lt. James Nicolson, who was the only member of Fighter Command to be awarded the Victoria Cross during WW2.

General aims – 1. Improving the finish and appearance of the model by eliminating joint lines, and boxing in the wheel wells. 2. Basic conversion involving change in colour scheme and markings.

Basic kit – Airfix Spitfire Mk. 1a.

Procedure – This is a very simple conversion. Basically, the model is built exactly as per the kit instructions. All interior detail should be fitted and painted before the fuselage halves are cemented together, as it is impossible to do a satisfactory job otherwise. Whether or not the modeller wishes to super-detail

Spitfire Mk.1a, K9942 on display at Horse Guards Parade London. This machine can be seen in the RAF Museum at Hendon.

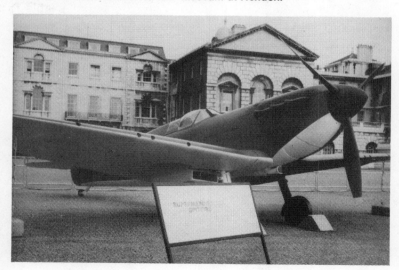

the cockpit area is a matter of taste or modelling skill, and strictly falls outside the scope of this particular section. Suffice it to say that photo-etched accessories are now available to super-detail a 1:72 scale Spitfire cockpit, and cut down on the work which previously involved using pieces of scrap plastic and heat stretched sprue.

A simple process such as boxing in the wheel wells to prevent a see through look will greatly improve the finish of the completed model. There are two ways of doing this, so it's a matter of finding the method that best suits the model you are building. One method is to use thin plastic card, cut and folded to conform with the outline of the wheel wells. Any excess plastic protruding from the wheel wells can then be cut away, and final adjustments made with wet 'n' dry paper.

An alternative method is to cement pieces of scrap plastic around the outline of the wells on the inner surface of the lower wing. Make sure that they are not too prominent, otherwise the upper and lower wing may be prevented from meeting. After cementing the upper and lower wings together, the wheel well walls can be built up with filler, or other suitable substance such as plasticine. The scrap plastic previously positioned acts as an anchor if this method is used.

Once major components have had time to dry thoroughly, all

Boxing in wheel wells with plastic card. (Spitfire Vb wing, not to scale).

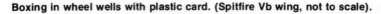

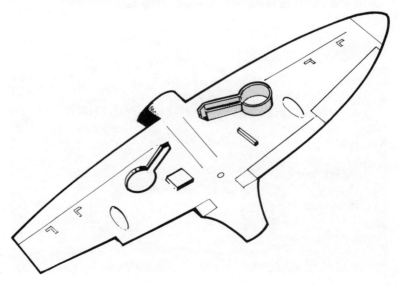

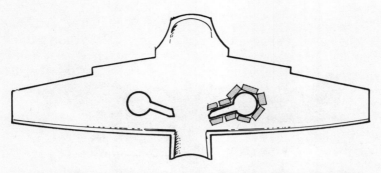

An alternative method of boxing in wheel wells. Pieces of scrap plastic are cemented around wheel well on inner surface of lower wing. (Spitfire 1a wing, not to scale).

traces of the joint lines should be removed. If these are particularly prominent, or if a step appears along the joint, filler may need to be used, or the joint filed down until it is possible to use various grades of wet 'n' dry paper to finish off the job.

Once the wings have been cemented to the fuselage, and the wheel wells boxed in, the undercarriage can be fitted, or it can be left off until later. The filing of small flats on the wheels helps give an impression of the weight of the aircraft and improves its "sit", rather than making it appear to be perched on grossly over inflated tyres. Incidentally, tyres are best painted a dark shade of grey rather than black.

Whenever possible, and the Spitfire is a case in point, I like to leave off items such as aerials, pitot tubes and transparencies etc. until last so as to minimise the possibility of their being knocked off or damaged. The canopy can be secured in position with PVA and any excess adhesive is also easily removed with a damp cloth or finger tip.

After the model has been completed, it should be set aside to dry for at least 24 hours before being carefully washed in warm, soapy water. This helps to remove grease and dust from the model's surface, but make sure that the water does not come into contact with any PVA which you may have used, otherwise it will dissolve. After the model has been dried, an undercoat of matt white or light grey (depending on the scheme in which the model is to be finished) can then be applied. This also has the advantage of showing up any blemishes which can be dealt with at this stage.

The camouflage can now be applied. This consists of a disruptive pattern of dark green and dark earth on the upper

Spitfire Mk. 1a, K9942 as modelled by the author.

surfaces, with the port undersurfaces being finished in black, and the starboard undersurfaces in white, the demarcation being along the aircraft's centre line. Masking tape can be used to achieve a hard demarcation line between the colours on the upper and lower surfaces, and in this case between the colours on the undersurface. The spinner and propeller are both black, the latter with 4 in. yellow tips.

Before the decals are applied, I like to give my models a coat of gloss varnish which helps to eliminate the appearance of unsightly carrier film around the decals. Gloss varnish should also be applied if the Microscale system is to be used. Very simply, this is a technique which eliminates carrier film from around the decals, and gives them a painted-on appearance.

The decals themselves can be taken from the decal bank, or an appropriate Modeldecal sheet, and consist of 40 in. diameter Type B wing roundels, and 30 in. Type B fuselage roundels. The Squadron codes are medium sea grey, and are 24 in. high, with the rear fuselage serial in 8 in. high black characters. No fin flash was carried, this being replaced by the pre-war style of displaying the squadron badge of a bird in flight on a white arrowhead. This item was a rub down decal, and came from the decal bank.

Finally, the decals were sealed with a 50/50 mix of gloss and matt varnish which gives a nice sheen, and is particularly suitable for a preserved machine such as this. However, operational aircraft would have a worn and weathered appearance. As a finishing touch, the port and starboard wing tip navigation lights are painted red and green respectively.

Spitfire Mk. IIa, P7350—this belongs to the Battle of Britain Memorial Flight.

CONVERSION 2

Subject – Spitfire Mk. IIa P7665, YT-L, of No.65 (East India) Sqn. as it appeared in January 1941.

General aims – 1. Cross kitting and/or use of the spares box. 2. Markings from the decal bank, or from specialist decal sheets.

Basic kit – Airfix Spitfire Mk. 1a.

Procedure – To all intents and purposes, the Mk. II version of the Spitfire was a Mk. 1 airframe fitted with a more powerful Merlin XII engine. Consequently, the only external feature to distinguish the Mk. II from the Mk. 1 was a small blister on the starboard side of the nose immediately behind the spinner of the Mk. IIs. This blister covered the redesigned reduction gear which was fitted to the Merlin XII engine, and should be featured on every Mk.II model. All other aspects of construction should be as per the Mk.1 already described.

A simple way of portraying the teardrop-shaped blister is to cement a short length of plastic rod in position, and then build up the blister with body putty. When this has hardened, the blister can be simulated by carving away excess material with a knife, followed by the use of wet 'n' dry until the desired shape is arrived at.

This particular aircraft had the more rounded Rotol propeller and spinner fitted. This may be taken from the spares box as in

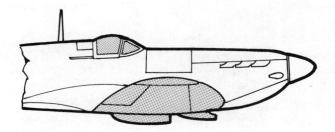

Spitfire Mk.II profile. Note bulge over Coffman Cartridge starter and Rotol spinner, 1:72 scale.

this case, or from the Airfix Series 2 kit of the Hurricane 1, which in turn could be built as a machine fitted with a de Havilland propeller and spinner which is now left over from the Spitfire kit. There are plenty of photographic references of Hurricanes thus fitted.

This Spitfire was finished in dark green and dark earth on its upper surfaces, with sky undersurfaces, including the rear fuselage band and spinner. All decals came from the Modeldecal range, apart from the Squadron's presentation name, which was a rub down transfer from the decal bank, and

The author's completed Mk.IIa—a simple conversion to effect.

consist of the following dimensions – 56 in. Type B upper wing roundels, 45 in. Type A underwing roundels, with a 35 in. diameter Type A1 on the fuselage. The Squadron codes are 24 in. high, and in sky. The fin flash extends the full height of the fin, and is 18 in. wide, each colour being equal in width. Again, the decals were sealed with a coat of varnish. The completed model can then be discretely weathered if desired.

CONVERSION 3

Subject – Spitfire Mk. 1a, K9795 of No. 19 Squadron as it appeared on October 31st, 1938, when the squadron displayed its aircraft to the press.

General aims – 1. Cross kitting and using specialist decal sheets. 2. Using practical techniques involved in modifying canopies.

Basic kit – Airfix Spitfire Mk. 1a.

Procedure – A very simple conversion, this time involving the use of parts from another kit, or of commercially available accessories. Construction involves the same steps as those already described for K9942, including the boxing in of the wheel wells, but with the following modifications.

Early Spitfire 1s, such as K9795, were fitted with a fixed pitch

Spitfire Mk.1a, K9795 which requires only minor modifications to the Airfix kit.

two-bladed wooden propeller. For this conversion, this item was taken from the Hasegawa Spitfire 1 kit, which provides it as an alternative along with a three-bladed propeller. If you do not have this kit, then a suitable propeller can be found in the Aeroclub range of accessories. The kit aerial has to be modified to the 'pole' variety, or replaced with a suitable length of plastic rod.

At this stage in its career, K9795 was fitted with the early style of canopy windscreen without the external bulletproof glass which was later fitted to Spitfires, and which is a feature of the Airfix kit canopy. Two canopies are supplied in the Hasegawa kit, including the earlier style, but neither will fit the Airfix kit without recourse to some surgery in the cockpit area. The answer therefore, is to modify the Airfix canopy to represent the earlier style.

This is done by removing the external bulletproof windscreen with a sharp knife. Then the windscreen area is gently sanded until it is flat in relation to its side panels. When you are satisfied with its shape, the next step is to restore its clarity. To do this, rub toothpaste with your finger onto the treated area. This is then wiped away, and the cockpit buffed vigorously with a piece of cloth or denim.

If the windscreen has been correctly modified, a small gap should appear between its bottom and the surface on which it should rest. This will be filled when the canopy is fitted in place with PVA adhesive. When this has dried, the complete canopy can be given a coat of clear varnish which restores the clarity of its surface. You could, of course, apply the varnish before the canopy is fitted in place.

Painting the framework on transparencies can be a tricky business. To simplify the process, you can use masking agents such as Humbrol's *Maskol* which is applied over the transparency apart from the framework itself. This can then be painted, and when dry, the masking agent peeled away. Another method is to paint strips of sellotape in the appropriate colour, and then to cut very narrow strips which are placed over the canopy's framework. This sounds much more difficult than it really is, and the results can be quite impressive.

The colour scheme of the model consists of dark green and dark earth uppers, with silver undersurfaces. Prominent style roundels of the Type A1 variety with yellow surrounds were carried on camouflaged surfaces, and were 56 in. in diameter on the wings, and 35 in. on the fuselage. The underwing roundels were 50 in. diameter Type A. The serial was carried on the wing undersurfaces in 12 in. high black characters, and face forward on the port wing, and towards the trailing edge of the starboard wing. The serial was also repeated on the rear fuselage in 8 in. high black characters.

The Squadron number 19 was painted on the fin for the taking of the press photographs in flight colours, which were yellow in the case of K9795. Unless a suitable decal can be found, the answer is to apply a close match, or modify a decal to the appropriate style. This can then be hand-painted in the appropriate colour.

CONVERSION 4

Subject – Spitfire Mk. IIb, P8332, ZD–L, of No. 222 Sqn., May-August 1941.

General aims – Conversion involving major cross kitting.

Basic kits – Airfix Spitfire Mk. 1a and Spitfire Mk. Vb.

Procedure – Very early in the war, it was realised that the aircraft of Fighter Command would have to be armed with a heavier armament than that of 8 × 0.303 in. machine guns in order to bring down their adversaries, which were beginning to carry increased armour protection. To pack a heftier punch, 2 × 20 mm cannons were mounted, one in each wing, along

A major cross-kitting exercise is needed to build this Spitfire Mk.IIb.

with 4 × 0.303 in. machine guns, the other four being replaced by the cannons. In order to differentiate between the cannon armed Spitfires and those which carried the "standard" armament, the latter were retrospectively designated as having the "a" wing armament, while the cannon armament was known as the "b" wing. Indeed, as the Spitfire was developed, further armament designations were added, but that's another story!

The work involved in producing the Mk. IIb basically involves grafting the Mk. Vb wings on to the Mk. 1a fuselage. However, the aileron hinge lines on the wing uppersurfaces of the Vb are wrongly positioned, and need to be corrected. New aileron hinge lines should be scored with a sharp knife using a steel rule as a straight edge. This modification should be carried out to every model which is fitted with the Airfix Spitfire Vb wing (see below). I find it easier to do this before joining the upper and lower wings. The old hinge line can now be filled in, and when dry, sanded flat. Any surface detail which is lost in the surrounding areas while the filler is sanded down, can then be restored, again by using a sharp knife and a steel rule.

The next task is to remove the small bulges above the wheel wells. This is achieved through the use of a file, followed by progressively finer grades of wet 'n' dry paper, until all trace is removed.

For this conversion, the Mk. 1a fuselage is used, together with the propeller and spinner supplied in the Mk. 1 kit. As already stated and described in the Mk. IIa conversion, a small teardrop shaped bulge has to be added to the starboard engine cowling just behind the spinner. This is a feature of every Spitfire Mk. II.

Before the wings are cemented in place, they should be

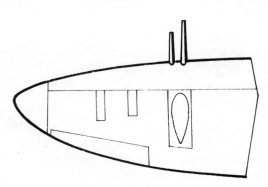

Modified aileron hinge line and armament configuration of twin cannon armed Mk.Vc's, 1:72 scale.

offered to the fuselage dry to check for fit. Minor adjustments may have to be made with a knife and wet 'n' dry paper to achieve a satisfactory fit. Frequent dry runs are recommended to ensure that too much plastic is not removed.

If filler is required in the wing/fuselage joint, then it should be applied sparingly, as it makes the excess easier to remove when the treated area is sanded to shape. The remainder of the kit may now be completed with the parts taken from the Spitfire Mk. 1a kit.

Once the undercoat has been applied, and any resulting blemishes dealt with, the camouflage scheme of dark green/dark brown uppers and sky undersurfaces, together with a sky spinner and rear fuselage band may be applied. The squadron codes are in sea grey medium, and came from the Modeldecal range, as did the roundels, fin flash, and serial number.

This particular aircraft was a presentation machine, and carried the legend "Soebang" in small, presumeably white, characters on the cowling forward of the cockpit. Suitable decals were found in the Almark range. Because of their small size, the letters making up the presentation name were applied first of all to a piece of clear decal, and then sealed with gloss varnish. When dry, this was applied to both sides of the cowling in the same manner as is used with a commercially produced decal. A coat of satin varnish seals the decals, and gives a characteristic sheen to the model. Weathering and staining can then be applied if desired.

CONVERSION 5

Subject – Spitfire Vc BR344 as it appeared on May 9th 1942 before flying off USS *Wasp* to reinforce Malta.

General aims – Conversion involving modification and basic improvements, together with the use of resin accessories and items from the spares box.

Basic kit – Airfix Spitfire Vb.

Procedure – Of all the Spitfires produced the Mk. V was the most numerous, being produced in a, b and c wing armament configuration. Several Mk. Vs were tropicalised by the fitting of a large and bulky looking filter beneath the nose for use in

Desert camouflage on this Spitfire Vc certainly makes a refreshing change from the usual brown and green schemes.

dusty or tropical areas. The subject of this conversion, BR344, had the tropical filter fitted, and was armed with 4×20 mm cannon. Because of the armanent which it carried, BR344 had the large style blisters on its cannon bay access panel.

Most of the work involved in converting the Vb into a Vc is to the wings and is as follows:

1 Remove the blisters on the wing upper surface above the wheel wells and sand smooth.

2 Remove the cannon bulges above and below the wings.

3 Cement blanking plates from thin plastic card on the inner surfaces of the wings, and fill in the holes left after removing the blisters with your favourite brand of filler. When dry, this can be sanded smooth to the contours of the surrounding area.

4 Scribe new aileron hinge lines in the correct position on the wing upper surfaces and fill in the old aileron hinge line.

5 Cement together upper and lower wings.

6 Box in wheel wells.

7 The inner machine-gun access panel detail on the wing upper surface should be removed, and a new access panel scribed in its correct position.

8 As this particular aircraft carried 4×20 mm cannon, it is logical to assume that its machine guns were not fitted in order to save weight. In this case, both the machine-gun port and cartridge ejector chutes would have been sealed to prevent the ingress of dirt. Photographs of BR433 do not clarify this point, but we can safely assume that this was the case. Accordingly, the machine-gun ports and ejector chutes were filled in and sanded smooth. At the same time the Vb style cannon ejector chutes was also filled in and sanded smooth. The Vb cannon ejector chutes is located just outboard and to the rear of both wheel wells. While correct for the Vb, it is incorrect for the Vc. New ejector chutes were simulated from strips of black decal after all painting had been completed.

9 New cannon access panel bulges now need to be constructed, and great care must be taken to ensure that they are correctly positioned, so a study of plans and relevant photographs is strongly recommended. The new blister can be built up from suitably shaped pieces of thin plastic card built up one upon the other. The first strip of plastic card to be positioned should be the same size and shape as the cannon blister. Each successive layer built up on the first should be slightly smaller until the correct height has been reached, when body putty is used over the strips to form the blister itself. When it has hardened, the body putty can be sanded to shape. The number of strips needed to build up the blister will of course depend upon the thickness of plastic card used (see below).

10 When the cannon blister has been shaped, the outline of the access panel can be carefully scribed with a sharp knife and a steel rule used as a straight edge.

11 The fuselage can be constructed at any time, or as a break while the wings are dealt with. The fuselage is completed as per

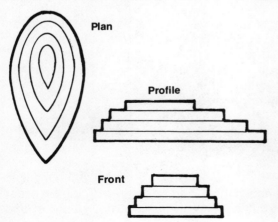

Plan

Profile

Front

Plan and profile views of method used to build up shape of cannon blister with strips of plastic (not to scale).

the kit instructions apart from the propeller and spinner which are consigned to the spares box, and suitable items taken from the Spitfire 1a, or the spares box, substituted in their place.

12 Once the wings have been cemented to the fuselage and the joint cleaned up, the tailplanes can be positioned.

13 The large, chin mounted tropical filter which replaces the kit's carburettor air intake came from the Airkit Enterprise range of resin items. This comes in two halves, and either instant glue or a five minute epoxy adhesive is used to glue the parts together, and also, to fix resin items in position. Once the location pegs for the carburettor intake had been removed, the new resin tropical filter proved to be a nice snug fit.

14 This particular aircraft was armed with 4×20 mm cannons, so another set of cannons will have to be taken from a second kit, or fabricated from plastic rod. The new cannons are located either side of the location hole in the Vb's wing leading edge. This is filled in and new location holes opened up with a pin vice and a small drill of suitable diameter. It should be noted that the outer cannon is shorter in length than the inner one.

15 The reminder of the kit may now be completed as per the instructions. The subject of the conversion was finished in the 'desert' scheme of dark earth and mid-stone uppers, with azure blue undersurfaces. The serial number and roundels came from the Modeldecal range. The unusual letter–number fuselage code is in white, and proved to be more difficult to obtain.

Finally, a suitable number was found on an Almark *Luftwaffe*

Another view of the author's Spitfire Vc conversion.

The Royal Swedish Air Force Spitfire PRXIX finished in overall PRU Blue.

Sheet (No. *A13*). While the letter came from the decal bank. If decals are not available for the codes, then suitable decals could be adapted for use and overpainted if necessary. An alternative method would be to paint the codes on a piece of transparent decal and then apply this to the model.

CONVERSION 6

Subject – Spitfire PR XIX of the initial batch of six aircraft supplied to the Royal Swedish Air Force as it appeared at Chilbolton, prior to delivery in October 1948.

General aims – Practising techniques involved in working with vacformed kits, and white metal accessories.

Basic kit – Aeroclub F XIV vacformed fuselage, white metal accessories, and Airfix Spitfire Mk. 1a wings.

Procedure – The PR XIX was the ultimate specialist PR version of the Spitfire to be developed, and the sole PR version to be powered by the Rolls-Royce Griffon engine. To this version goes the distinction of flying the RAF's last operational Spitfire sortie, in Malaya, on April 1st, 1954, and the last Spitfire sortie with the RAF in 1957 as part of the Woodvale Met. Flight. Currently, three PR XIXs are maintained in airworthy condition by the Battle of Britain Memorial Flight.

Many modellers are put off attempting construction of a vacformed kit because of their more complex appearance when compared to the more traditional injection moulded kits. True, some of these are in the "experienced modeller" bracket, but there are several kits around on which modellers can cut their teeth. The basis of the following conversion was the Aeroclub Spitfire F XIVc fuselage, and the plans for the PR XIX which appear in *Aircraft Archive Fighters of World War Two Vol. 1* by **Argus Books**, proved invaluable.

The Aeroclub parts come on a single sheet of plastic, and the first step is to remove, and prepare the fuselage halves. Carefully score around each part with a sharp knife, applying more pressure with each cut, until the parts can be snapped from their backing sheet.

Next, clean up the surfaces to be mated together of the residue plastic from the backing sheet, so that a smooth, even surface is obtained. There are alternative methods whereby this can be achieved. One is to tape a piece of wet 'n' dry paper to a flat surface, and rub the parts on this in a smooth, circular motion, making sure that even pressure is applied along the length of the part. Another method is to wrap a piece of wet 'n' dry around a block of balsa, and work along the surfaces to be rubbed down. Frequent checks are essential to ensure that too much plastic is not removed. Pay particular attention to the rudder, to achieve as thin a trailing edge as possible.

The cockpit area can now be opened up by removing the surplus plastic from this area. Take care not to remove too much as final adjustments can be made later on. The underside of the fuselage where the wing is to be located can also be opened up at this stage. Again, final adjustments can be made later on.

Before the fuselage halves are cemented together, small strips of plastic card should be cemented to the inside of one fuselage so that it protrudes beneath the edge which forms the fuselage joint. This provides a surface for the other fuselage half to rest on, and makes for a much stronger joint. The fuselage halves can now be cemented together with a mixture of tube and liquid cement, and set aside until the joint has dried thoroughly, when it can be cleaned up in the usual manner.

The wings can be dealt with at this stage. These came from the Airfix Spitfire Mk. 1a, and were left over from a previous conversion. The PR XIX was unarmed, so use of the Mk. 1a wings cuts down on the work involved. To begin with, the upper and lower wings are cemented together and the wheel wells boxed in. Next, the machine-gun ports in the wing leading edge, and the cartridge ejector chutes are filled in, and sanded smooth when dry.

The panel lines on the upper wing surfaces depicting the machine-gun access panels were removed with a sharp knife, as were the bulges over the wheel wells, and then sanded smooth. Similarly, all raised detail on the wing undersurfaces was also removed. When all sanding had been completed, the treated area was given a wash of liquid cement (albeit carefully!) which eliminates the scratch marks. Using the plans as references, relevant panel lines were then rescribed with a sharp knife and a steel rule.

The cockpit was then detailed and painted through the fuselage underside. An instrument panel was found in the spares box, and modified to fit. The pilot's seat and control column also came from the spares box, and were cemented onto a piece of plastic card which acted as the cockpit floor. This in turn was cemented to the fuselage, ensuring that the seat was correctly positioned while so doing. The detailing of the cockpit gave rigidity to the fuselage structure.

The wings were then offered to the fuselage, and the benefit of not removing too much plastic from the fuselage earlier on can now be appreciated. The area to be removed to accomodate the wings was carefully marked out, and then opened up. The wings were regularly offered to the fuselage at this stage to check the fit.

Once a satisfactory fit was arrived at, small retaining strips of plastic were cemented inside the fuselage where the wings rest. These act as 'steps' for the wings, and provide a better base on which they can rest.

The wings were then cemented in the fuselage with tube and liquid cement, and placed in a home made jig to ensure that they remained in the correct position in relation to the fuselage while they dried.

When the wing/fuselage assembly had thoroughly dried, the joint was examined and treated with filler as necessary. This was then sanded so that the end result was a smooth, flowing joint between the wings and the fuselage.

Turning to the undersurfaces, the fairing for the wing tank booster pump, immediately forward of the wheel well, was constructed in exactly the same manner as used for the Coffman starter cartridge bulge on the Mk. II conversion.

The small fairing, outboard of the wheel wells was simulated by floating a thin piece of plastic rod into position with liquid cement. When this had hardened, its leading and trailing edges were sanded to produce an aero-dynamically clean teardrop outline. The beam approach aerial on the fuselage undersurface was simulated in the same manner.

The Aeroclub radiators were prepared in the same manner as the fuselage. Blanking plates, cut from scrap plastic, were cemented inside the radiators to prevent a see through appearance before they were cemented in place. Any gaps along the wing/radiator joint line can be filled in later on.

The tailplanes also came from the spares box. The type fitted to the PR XIX had the enlarged elevator horn balance, so the Airfix items have to be modified. A new elevator horn balance line is scribed, and the unwanted line is filled in and sanded smooth.

The locating tabs were then removed, and the tailplanes butt joined in position with tube and liquid cement. Make sure that the tailplanes are aligned by making visual checks from all angles. When satisfied with their positioning, they can be set in a jig while they dry.

The PR XIX had an air intake located below the exhaust manifolds on the port side for its pressurised cockpit. Working from the plans, this was simulated by cutting a piece of an axle from a WW1 fighter, now in the spares box, to the desired length. Its trailing edge was then sanded to a taper, and this then glued in position with liquid cement.

Aeroclub also provide white metal parts which include the carburettor air intake, undercarriage, and the propeller and spinner. This is a soft material to work with, and poses no problems. Each part should be cleaned and prepared with a fine metal file, and fixed in place with instant glue.

Working from the plans, and using photographs as references, the carburettor air intake was fitted in place. Adjustments with a file were necessary, and to the nose area, before a satisfactory fit was achieved.

The main undercarriage legs were dealt with next, and their fit posed no problems. However, as provided, the main wheels have the three spoke hubs, while the subject of the conversion had the four spoke wheels fitted, so suitable wheels were taken from the Aeroclub range of accessories. Again, small flats should be filed on the wheels to simulate the aircraft's weight.

Before the tailwheel was fitted, a location hole was opened up with a pin vice and suitable diameter bit. After positioning the tailwheel, doors for the rear wheel well were cut from thin plastic card and cemented in place. The propeller and spinner were cleaned up and fitted in place after a small hole had been opened up to accept the propeller shaft.

The canopy should be fitted after painting has been completed, but is dealt with here for convenience. The canopy provided with the F XIV fuselage is the fighter style. The canopy is carefully removed from its carrier sheet, with a pair of scissors and offered to its position to check for fit, adjustments being made as necessary. Then, the windscreen was carefully removed as it has to be replaced with the rounded style, PR windscreen. This was cut from another PR canopy which also came from the Aeroclub range. Unfortunately, it is not possible to use this canopy as it is, as it is the variety fitted with the side blisters, and therefore not suitable for the PR XIX. The new windscreen was found to be a very satisfactory fit, and no problems were encountered in mating it with the rest of the canopy. The framework on the canopy may be simulated with narrow strips of painted sellotape.

Finally, the pitot tube was cemented in place, and the complete model painted light grey, which served to highlight any blemishes, and as an undercoat for the overall PRU Blue colour scheme. The propeller blades were painted black with 4 in. yellow tips, exhausts rust and tyres a dark shade of grey. The camera ports were simulated by hand-painted black discs, or they could be cut from a decal sheet.

The Swedish roundels came from the decal bank, while the aircraft's fuselage number was modified from the Modeldecal range. As the serial number was so small as to be illegible in 1:72 scale, it was omitted. A coat of gloss varnish was then applied which served to seal the decals in place and represent the sheen which was so typical of many PR aircraft.

3 HIGH-TECH AND MIXED MATERIAL KITS

PETE LOOPER

In addition to the standard plastic kit there has now evolved the 'Hi-Grade' or 'High-Tech' super-detailed kit, aimed at the upper end of the market. They have only recently arrived on the scene and may be unfamiliar to many modellers with their additional white metal and etched metal parts. This chapter aims to describe what these kits really offer, where problems can arise during their construction and how to obtain maximum realism from these and normal kits.

There have already been many High-Tech car and motorcycle kits, most notably from Gunze Sangyo, who have now also released their first High-Tech armour kits; but the aircraft kit market has only just received attention with this type of kit. Hasegawa was one of the first manufacturers to release Hi-Grade aircraft kits when they re-released some of their earlier kits with added extras and an increase in price of around £10–15. This huge price difference has deterred many modellers from purchasing them and many arguments have raged as to whether they are really worth the extra cost. High-Grade kit production must be a worthwhile prospect for model manufacturers as more of them are turning to this type of kit as their top-of-the-range product.

The first Hasegawa Hi-Grade kits were updated and modified from their older kits and here a few problems arose because when any new parts are used on an older kit, the basic model may not be up to today's high standards. The first Hasegawa Hi-Grade kit that had double-standard mouldings was the Focke-Wulf Fw190D-9; new fuselage halves, a cowling and canopy of excellent quality were provided but the wings, tailplanes and undercarriage doors came directly from the Hasegawa Fw190A kit that must be at least 20 years old! Whereas the new parts are smooth and nicely engraved, the older parts are quite different with raised-line detail and masses of rivets.

Any self-respecting modeller would be unhappy with this contrast in quality and the only course of action available is to

Peter Looper's beautifully constructed Fw 190D-9. This Hasegawa Hi-Grade kit still utilises parts from the original Fw 190A kit which had heavy surface detail. Therefore, the wings and tailplanes have been sanded smooth and re-scribed to bring them up to the standard of the rest of the kit.

remove all of the older detail by sanding it off and then re-scribing the detail to match the quality of the new parts. This extra work may sound a daunting prospect to some modellers who have little experience in this area but it is not really too difficult to accomplish.

The techniques employed to re-scribe the older parts to make them look like new have been around since the start of plastic models as we know them. It has taken many years for accessory manufacturers to recognise the need for scribing tools and templates but this has recently been taken care

Trimaster scribing templates and saws (saws in centre).

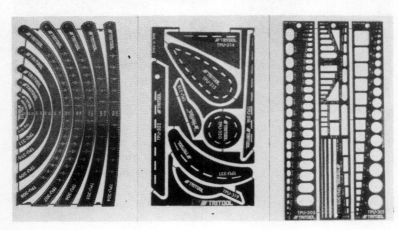

of by Trimaster and Verlinden Productions. Scribing plastic is rarely a clean and simple task as the scribing tool, or needle, does not cut the plastic but rather ploughs a trough that leaves slightly raised edges. The traditional method is to lightly scribe the surface and then repeat until the desired line depth is reached; the surface is then restored with very fine wet and dry paper and then the scribed lines are cleaned out again. This technique is satisfactory for straight lines but when it comes to complex panels, piano hinges and vents the modeller is usually forced to hunt around for something to use as a template.

The Trimaster range is rapidly expanding and it includes a large variety of items to enable just about any panel line to be scribed; there are circles, ovals, rectangles, triangles and squares in many different sizes and the etched metal templates are thin enough to bend around kit parts. Another set of templates allows the modeller to scribe straight lines around a curved surface; each of these curved templates has a row of holes around the edge that allows rivet details to be added if desired. The Verlinden templates are similar to the first Trimaster set but they also include access panel shapes, louvred grilles, formation lights and piano hinges in addition to the normal selection of ovals, squares and circles.

There just remains to decide what to use as a scriber. A

Verlinden Productions' 1:48 scale scribing template.

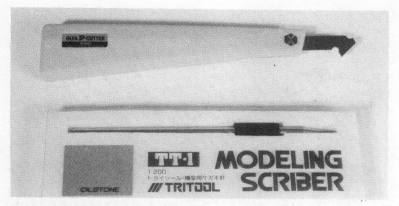

Olfa and Trimaster scribing tools.

compass needle held firmly in a pin vice is a good and readily available tool as is the custom-made Trimaster Modeling Scriber. These are well suited to the task but, when it comes to scribing straight lines, the most effective tool is the Olfa P-Cutter with a blade that is pulled backwards across the plastic. Instead of causing a furrow on the surface, it actually cuts the plastic and leaves a straight line without the need for any laborious sanding. If any lines overshoot their intended destinations, a drop of cyanoacrylate super glue can be used to seal the error and this can be easily sanded smooth ready for re-scribing to the correct point.

Since Hasegawa's first releases in their Hi-Grade range there have been more manufacturers eager to produce this type of kit such as Trimaster and Fujimi. These two manufacturers have released all-new high quality kits that, thankfuly, do not need any scribing work to bring them up to standard; the Hasegawa Hi-Grade range has dramatically improved since their earliest releases and it is good to see that their later kits, like the RAF Phantoms, are almost completely new and do not suffer from the mixed quality problems of some of their earlier releases.

'High-Tech' kits offer many new parts in materials other than plastic and these may cause some problems due to unfamiliarity, or because they are difficult to work with. The white metal parts are generally used for items like aircraft undercarriage and propellers, car chassis and tank hull castings. These parts are normally of a really high standard and, generally, the more a kit costs, the better the quality of the white metal accessories.

Box illustration for Hasegawa's Hi-Grade British FG1 Phantom in colourful A&AEE Boscombe Down markings.

The main advantage of white metal over plastic is that it has more strength enabling thin true-to-scale thicknesses to be produced rather than an over-scale plastic part. A white metal casting's surface is not super-smooth and the mould itself may have left tiny amounts of flash or imperfections. Any flash or mould lines must therefore be removed carefully with a small file. A coat of self-etch primer is usually the best way to achieve a smooth finish prior to the parts being painted in their correct colours.

Many of the metal parts will need to be glued together before painting and a fast acting super glue is usually the best adhesive for this; a pin vice and a selection of small drills will be of great use during the construction of the white metal parts where they are used to open up locating holes or to accentuate the finer details. If the metal parts can be glued together before any painting is carried out then the task is much easier and the resulting assembly is much stronger. There are many alternative adhesives for white metal parts such as Araldite Rapid, Bostik Hyperbond and Micro Liquatape. The last mentioned adhesive is extremely versatile and can be used on almost any area of a model where great bonding strength is not required. Parts that are difficult to hold can be pre-positioned with a drop of Liquatape as it is a clear contact adhesive with the same qualities as white school glue when it is wet. A thin

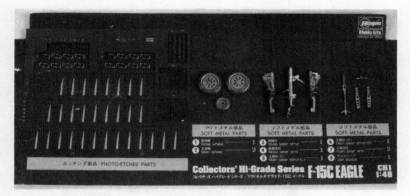

Hi-Grade accessories from Hasegawa's 1:48 scale F-15C Eagle.

coat of Liquatape is applied to one part and it is left to dry until it is no longer a milky white colour but clear. The parts to be joined are then held together and, when the positioning is correct, a small amount of pressure is applied to hold them in place. If the parts are under any tension, or if higher strength is required, then a small amount of super glue can be used to strengthen the bond and make it really permanent.

Oleo struts on aircraft can be polished to a high gloss metal finish by rubbing the white metal parts with the straight side of a household sewing needle; this burnishes the metal easily and the resulting finish is very realistic and mimics highly polished chrome steel. To prevent the metal from oxidising a thin coat of acrylic varnish should be brushed on to the polished areas to seal the metal; acrylic varnish dries very quickly and allows the work to progress without delays, it dries crystal clear and is not subject to yellowing with age. Any brake pipes supplied with a 'High-Tech' kit are best attached with Liquatape initially and finally fixed with super glue afterwards as they can be really troublesome to fit.

Another type of accessory included in 'High-Tech' kits are those made from etched metal. The metal used can either be brass or stainless steel and some of the parts can be very difficult to fit in place on the model. A sharp pair of snips will cut the parts from their frame and the small sharp runners will need to be filed off before the parts are used. Many finely detailed parts are made from this material and their delicacy greatly improves the overall appearance of the finished model. If the parts are etched brass then they can easily be bent to follow the

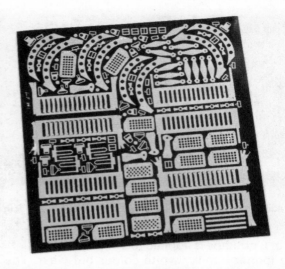

IPMS USA—P-51 Mustang etched metal detail pieces in 1:24 scale.

curve of a canopy, but with stainless steel the material is often too hard to flex satisfactorily.

The use of Liquatape on parts that are under tension is not always successful and other methods need to be employed; one useful tip used by some modellers is to apply thin double-sided tape onto the etched metal part and then use a sharp scalpel to trim away the excess tape. The other backing paper is then removed and the part is pressed onto the correct location; when it is where it should be, a small amount of super glue is run around the edge of the part to permanently seal it. Flat parts are not prone to any of these problems and they can simply be fitted with super glue from the start.

Many 'High-Tech' kits provide etched metal instrument panels that need to be carefully painted and the instruments are usually decals fitted behind acetate sheet 'glass'. I have had difficulty painting the etched metal instrument panels as the etching depth is very small. Although I have quite a steady hand with a paintbrush, I rarely achieve a satisfactory finish so, after extensive experimentation, my preferred method is to paint the entire panel with Tamiya acrylic Gloss Black paint and let it completely dry, The panel base colour, usually light grey, is then airbrushed over this using Xtracolor gloss enamel paint. The paint is left to dry for a day or two and then the panel is gently rubbed with a clean tissue dipped in white spirit; the

Waldron radio front panels and cockpit data plates in 1:32 scale.

gloss grey from the raised bezels and panels is progressively worn away leaving sharply defined black areas. The black bezels and panels should be almost perfectly finished after this process, but there may be very small amounts of touching-up to do until one is satisfied with the result.

If problems occur and the panel is spoilt, then all of the paint can be removed by soaking it in Methyl-Ethyl-Ketone (MEK) and using an old toothbrush to scrub away the paint so that the process can be started again. It may seem long-winded and time consuming, but the results can be very pleasing and far superior to brush painting. If the real panel is entirely black then a light dry-brushing with steel or grey coloured paint will make it look natural and also accentuate the finer details. Once the panel has been finished a spray coat of matt or semi-matt varnish tones down the panel to a more natural sheen.

When the main cockpit area has been completed the ejection seats or bucket seats can be fitted. Ejection seats are large and complex items that dominate most of the cockpit and they can make or break the overall effect of the model. A basic seat is normally included in the kit but some manufacturers, notably Monogram and Hasegawa, take extra care when they produce these parts. Good reference material on ejection seats is available and modellers should seek this out before building a kit; even the same type of seat may vary between different aircraft types such as the ACES II seat of the F-16 which differs noticeably from the same type of seat fitted to the F-15 and A-10. There are many actuating rods, handles and assorted modules on an ejection seat and these should be added to the seat where required and dry-brushed to let the detail be seen. Seat belts can be made from various materials such as paper, copper foil, masking tape or fine nylon sheet and the positioning of these belts should be carefully thought out.

So far I have only considered injection moulded plastic kits but there are also models produced from different materials, i.e. vacformed plastic and resin. Vacforms are dealt with elsewhere in this book, but the building of resin models falls within the bounds of this chapter. There are quite a good selection of resin models available in various scales and their quality varies from very poor to a very high standard. The cheaper kits are made from cast resin and they often have large amounts of flash around the parts; they come with only a few parts as the

Model Technologies' F-5E canopy detail set in 1:32 scale.

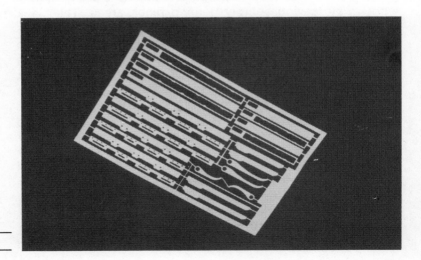

main bulk of the kit is made in one piece. The upper end of the resin kit market uses a similar moulding technique to standard kits where the resin is actually injection moulded. This enables a very fine finish to be achieved with the parts attached to a resin sprue like a normal kit.

Due to the use of more flexible moulds than injection moulded plastic kits, a resin model often appears ready built; some kits come complete with the wings and tailplanes already attached to the fuselage and only require the more delicate items to be attached to complete them. As the main aim of this chapter is to describe 'High-Tech' kits, a state-of-the-art resin kit was obtained as a comparison between these and standard kits. The kit is a Japanese made Volks 'Heinkel He219' in 1:48 scale and it comes complete with Microscale decals, white metal accessories and also resin accessories.

The main aircraft is built from only eight parts and the finish is of a high standard with only a few blemishes and a rather prominent mould line to worry about. There are many different types and qualities of resin and the He219 uses a light blue coloured type that is flexible enough to work with but care must be taken with all resin kits to ensure that one does not cause the material to snap. It is only flexible up to a point and after this it snaps easily; the components are joined together with super glue and this forms an extremely strong joint.

The filling of join lines can be carried out with some more of this glue run into the joint and sanded smooth when dry. Milliput is another useful filler and it is well suited for use on resin kits. The surface of the resin can be scribed if required but it is more difficult than with normal plastic as it is more brittle; the best scribed lines are produced with the Olfa P-Cutter knife as it cuts the line smoothly without causing a furrow. Most resin models need sanding to achieve a really good finish and normal fine grade wet and dry paper can be used for this; the surface can be brought up to the standards of a plastic kit and one should try to do this at each stage during construction. Perhaps the most noticeable difference between resin and plastic kits is their weight. A resin kit is a solid, heavy and strong model and this can cause a few problems if the kit needs to balance on a tricycle undercarriage.

A little weight in the nose usually allows a plastic model to sit correctly, but with a resin kit it is not possible to fit any nose weights as there is no interior space available. There is nothing more frustrating than a 'tailsitter' so find out where the centre of gravity is before construction commences. If the parts are taped together and any accessories carefully laid on the model as close to their correct positions as possible, the balance point can easily be ascertained.

If the model proves to be tail heavy then some lightening work will be needed to remedy this; a tailplane assembly will be too thin to alter so the fuselage is where excess weight will have to be removed from. If the tailplane assembly is a separate part that is attached to the end of the fuselage, then it will be easy to do, but if not, the fuselage must be cut apart to gain access to the interior. Using a selection of drills, progressively remove the material and, once sufficient resin has been removed to balance the model, the fuselage can be glued back together and the join line filled and smoothed out.

Having dealt with the resin itself, one can now turn to the other items included in the kit and these are all extremely fine and delicate. The white metal accessories in the He219 are cleanly cast and there are no less than 33 of them. Most of these form the complex undercarriage assemblies but others include cockpit accessories, radar aerials and propellers. The cockpit bath, exhaust dampers, undercarriage doors, seats and radar scopes are all made from tan coloured resin and the detail on these parts has to be seen to be believed. Both instrument panels are cleanly formed in the cockpit bath assembly and these will need instruments from a specialist decal sheet or

Instrument bezels from Fotocut.

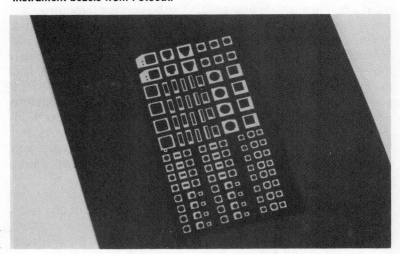

Waldron accessories to be fitted for maximum realism. The cockpit interior is so well detailed that virtually the only extras that it needs are two sets of seat belts and buckles. That just about sums up what a 'High-Grade' resin model offers; their price is quite high, but if the kit subject is one that really appeals then they are worth investigating.

Until now I have only considered kits with the super-detail accessories included but, over the last few years, more of the independent accessory producers have concentrated on etched metal items for a wide variety of subjects. Model Technologies, Waldron, PP Aeroparts, Fotocut and IPMS USA are just a few of the many companies that allow a standard kit to be improved with highly detailed etched metal accessories. Waldron produce photographically reproduced instruments that need a punch and die set to remove them from their sheet and these look very good in an instrument panel. Placards, oxygen pipes, seat belt buckles and rudder pedals are also included in their range and the modeller must weigh their cost against the kit itself and decide if this extra detail and complexity is really needed. With the very wide choice of accessories available it is very easy to spend twice the kit's retail price on the extras!

No matter how complex and expensive a kit may be, it will not

Waldron's punch and die set comes in a neat protective box.

look good if the modeller who builds it does not take time and care during every phase of its construction. Decals are possibly the most useful aids that a modeller has when it comes to making a model look authentic. Poorly painted anti-glare panels, de-icer boots, aerial covers and walkways can really spoil a model and items painted free-hand or with the aid of masking tapes often leave a step in the paintwork that looks wrong on a small model. For problem areas that need to be painted I use plain coloured decal sheet to eliminate the stepped or shaky-hand effect that detracts from the appeal of a model.

A few examples of how I use these decals is shown in the accompanying sketches and the results are worth the extra time spent on them. The decals are first carefully applied and then the remaining areas are filled in with a paintbrush; the paint must not reach the edge of the decal and it should flow smoothly over the area to blend the decal in and not let it show afterwards. Solid areas, such as Di-electric panels, can also be represented by decals and the use of solid silver decal sheet is ideal for areas on a natural metal or silver painted model where sharp demarcation lines are required.

Most models with a high gloss or pure matt finish look quite

(Left) To cut the front piece of decal, use a sharp scalpel blade around a suitably sized circle. Position this carefully and then bring the side pieces of decal strip up to it to produce a smooth outer line. When the decals are dry, paint over the complete anti-glare panel, being careful not to get too close to the edge of the decals. (Right) The interior is painted white or silver and the exterior colour is applied a little further inside than is required. A white or silver decal strip is then used to line the inside providing a sharp, clean demarcation line; this tip is of particular use on F-16 models.

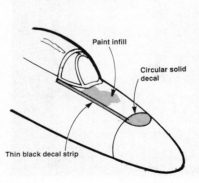

Paint infill

Circular solid decal

Thin black decal strip

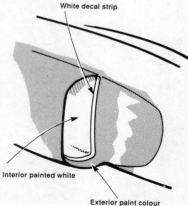

White decal strip

Interior painted white

Exterior paint colour

unrealistic, so some thought must be used to arrive at the perfect sheen for the model. This area of modelling can make all the difference; one should add a little gloss to a matt finish and spray a trial patch to assess the sheen. After a little experimentation the desired mix will be achieved and the entire model can be given an overall spray coat to seal the decals. Once the model has the correct finish it can be 'weathered' to look even more natural. This can add extra realism but one should be careful not to overdo things as too much can be worse than none at all. Reference to photographs of the actual machine being modelled is desirable but where these are not available a selection of the same machines should be studied to ascertain where the real thing leaks, loses paint or weathers.

A wartime machine is usually badly abused by the elements, weapon firing and hard combat use and models of actual fighting machines can stand quite heavy weathering. Peace-time machines, particularly aircraft, are the opposite and it takes years of service before they look old and worn. A modern jet fighter, pre-war biplane or an airliner can often appear only superficially dirty as their servicing crews take pride in their charges and endeavour to keep them in good condition;

Close-up of the finely etched metal intake grille on Hasegawa's 1:32 scale Hi-Grade Fw190D-9. It's almost a shame that the propeller and spinner have yet to go on!

US Naval aircraft are normally an exception and look in very poor condition paint-wise as their Corrosion Control Policy requires the panel joints to be sprayed over with fresh paint whenever they have been removed; this is very difficult to represent on a kit but care and perseverance at the task can reap their rewards and produce an unusual and exciting model.

The panel lines and other engraved details on a model often look better if they have been highlighted with a suitable colour and I prefer to use water soluble inks for this. When the glossed model has had the decals applied and they are properly dry, I run some thinned water-soluble grey ink into the panel lines and let it dry. Using a clean, moistened tissue, any residue on the surface is removed and the model is then studied to check that the desired effect has been achieved; if it doesn't look right it can be easily washed off and a lighter or darker shade re-applied until one is happy with it. The final varnish coat will permanently seal the ink in place and the weathering can be carried out on top of this; I always try to make a perfect factory-finish first and then weather them afterwards to achieve the required finish. Other methods involve the use of oil based paints, thinned enamels or even pastels, and every modeller

Visible through the open cockpit canopy on Hasegawa's Hi-Grade Fw190D-9 are the etched metal seat buckles.

will need to try the alternatives to find the one that pleases them most.

Patience and care are the main ingredients for successful modelling and a critical eye for detail will help one produce some excellent models; whether 'High-Tech' kits appeal to you or not is a matter of personal taste and financial constraints, but the extras that they include are now becoming very widespread on the accessory scene and the techniques peculiar to their construction are becoming quite common-place. As even newer materials are regularly reaching the modelling market, it may not be too long before the pure plastic kit disappears and the composite-material kit takes over; the 'High-Techs' may lead the way but the standard kits are striving to reach them and gain some of the limelight.

4   REFERENCE PHOTOGRAPHS FOR FUTURE MODELLING

JOHN HALE

There are many thousands of modellers who go no further than constructing a kit straight from the box, utilising the decals supplied; with the sophistication of modern kits, a most satisfactory result can be obtained. However, sooner or later the modeler will realise that the model which has been painstakingly constructed and finished will be identical to thousands of others that have come off the production line. The urge to build a model that is different, finished in the markings of an alternative unit, or slightly modified to represent a different mark, becomes strong.

To accomplish this, sources of reference are indispensable. While line drawings, or colour profiles to be found in books and magazines, have their uses, the best form of reference is a photograph of the subject to be modelled. Regrettably though, the accuracy of many drawings leaves a lot to be desired,

I try to photograph as many examples of unit markings as possible, such as this 237OCU badge on a Hunter, which shows evidence of a little repair work with the paintbrush.

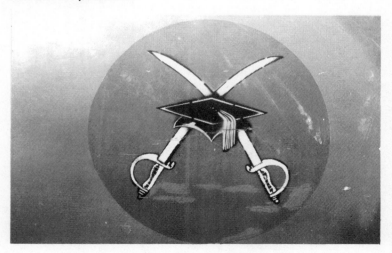

especially with regard to colour. Therefore, you can either purchase the necessary photographs in the form of slides or prints, or contained within books. However, the best route is to take the photographs yourself! Modelling a specific aircraft that you have seen in the flesh (or rather, aluminium!) greatly adds to the enjoyment of the hobby.

Circumstances in the UK are favourable to those modellers wishing to collate their own photographic resources. The price of photographic equipment, in relative terms, has never been lower, and it is possible to purchase a 35mm single lens reflex camera for the price of a couple of expensive kits. For novices in the field of cameras, a single lens reflex camera is one where the viewfinder is linked by mirrors to the lens, so that you see exactly what the lens sees.

Ancillary equipment, such as zoom lenses are also moderately priced. To become aware of what kind of equipment is available, buy a copy of a specialist photographic magazine and study the advertisements; then, go along to your local retailer and ask for a demonstration. There is also a wide choice of film available, both colour print and colour slide.

A wide range of accessories can be considered, such as flash guns, filters and tripods. It is suggested that only a basic kit be acquired at first: get to know how to handle your camera and lens, before branching out further. Photography, like modelling, becomes easier and better with more experience; only after gaining this experience should accessories be considered. For example, while I appreciate the advantages of using a tripod, I shall never use one as I already carry enough equipment around with me. A personal choice, of course: come to your own before you part with the cash!

Now that the modeller is fully equipped, the various opportunities for taking photographs should be considered, together with the type of photographs to be taken. I seem to take two types of photograph: overall views of the aircraft, showing the camouflage and markings scheme, and detail photographs of interesting parts of the airframe, squadron markings and other salient features. Make sure that you have identified your requirements before blazing away with the camera, as it is too late to realise that you have omitted to photograph some important detail when scrutinising your photographs a week or so later. And yes, I have made that mistake myself several times—so plan ahead! There are three main venues where such photographs can be taken; a) Air

Displays/Open Days, b) Museums, c) Operational airfields. These I have considered separately.

AIR DISPLAYS

These are arguably the most difficult places to take good reference photographs. Usually, the photographer is denied free and open access to the aircraft that are on static display. The modern world, with its ever present threat of terrorism and the actions of certain groups and factions, not to mention sheer wanton vandalism, has meant that the organisers of these events are unwilling to give the public freedom of access to the aircraft that they have come to see. The aircraft are thus almost invariably protected by a steel crowd barrier, or at least a rope. Often these are sufficiently close enough not to form an obstacle to the taking of detail shots.

A zoom lens is ideal for this kind of photography—often I use my 80-200mm lens in these situations. Difficulties may be met in taking shots of features on the underside of the aircraft due to the dense shadows, so use of a "fill in" flash may help. Certain parts of the airframe may prove to be beyond reach of the zoom lens, but again this problem is not insurmountable. A guard is almost invariably detailed to attend the aircraft, or the pilot or other aircrew members will be on hand to talk about their aircraft. A polite request to cross the barriers to take the required detail shot will often be favourably received.

While the taking of detail photographs can be carried out successfully at air displays, the prospects of taking good overall photographs of the whole aircraft can be slim. The presence of the crowd barriers can absolutely ruin any

A typical air display photograph: the steel barrier is nice, but that horrible F-5E spoils the background!

Reasonable results can sometimes be obtained, such as this Danish CF-104D at Mildenhall in May 1985.

photograph of the aircraft; another factor which may prevent the taking of good overall shots is the distressing tendency to cram as many aircraft as possible into the smallest space, packing them in wing-tip to wing-tip. The International Air Tattoo at Fairford suffers from such a complex, but it is by no means unique. Often, good photographs are completely impossible. The use of wide-angle lenses can sometimes overcome this situation, but as a personal matter I do not use any lens wider than 35mm (and this wide only as an emergency measure) due to the distorted effects produced thereby.

Extremely large crowds now attend most air displays in the UK, rendering it very difficult to photograph many aircraft without Auntie Nellie and all the kids being in your shot! There is very little that can be done about this, apart from either coming to the display early in the morning to avoid the crowds, or to stay to the end of the display and photograph the static aircraft when most of the public have gone home. Although the shots may be spoiled by the amounts of litter to be found on the floor, it is sometimes the better option of the two. Many air displays now have their own equivalent of the "Le Mans" start, with hundreds of photographers rushing in an attempt to take clear, uncluttered photographs. Often this is a forlorn hope due to the heavy presence of crowd barriers, and it appears that Auntie Nellie and the kids can move amazingly quickly too!

Compensating for the difficulties encountered in the static park, some air displays have an operational flightline in close proximity to the crowd line giving a precious opportunity to take some good, clear shots of aircraft taxying to and from their display routine. A telephoto or zoom lens are indispensable here. Two airfields which have this amenity are Mildenhall and Brawdy, but there are several others.

When it comes to taking good photographs of the aircraft in the flying display, the photographer is completely at the mercy of geography. Ideally, the crowdline should be positioned to the south of the runway, so that the sun will be behind the photographer. It is unfortunate that many first-class air displays are spoilt by making the crowd have to face into the sun during the display: Mildenhall is a prime example of this. The International Air Tattoo committee were fortunate when they had to change venue from Greenham Common to Fairford, as the latter location has the crowd positioned to the south of the runway, making it possible to take good photographs of the flying display all day long—that is, if the sun shines at all!

When attending a display which is not blessed with a south-side location, one can try to make the best of the situation and get to the end of the display axis: it may be possible to get shots of the aircraft turning at the end of their display run, so that one is not facing directly into the sun. Otherwise, one may try to leave the airfield and find a vantage point on the south side, although this is not always possible. Display aircraft may range in size from a C-5A Galaxy down to a Jet Provost, so a zoom lens is essential during a display. My personal equipment is an 80–200 mm zoom, together with a 300 mm telephoto lens for the smaller aircraft such as the F–16 or Hawk.

Often the crowd line is located such a long way from the runway that an even longer lens is required. Often the display aircraft are moving at such a speed that photography is very difficult, but they usually oblige with a couple of slow passes. It is important to "pan" the camera. To do this, lock on to the aircraft as it approaches, and continue to follow it until the desired shot is seen; squeeze the shutter release gently, still continuing to follow the aircraft through the viewfinder. Hopefully, a sharp photograph will result. Focussing may be difficult, so I pre-focus the lens on a selected spot on the runway rather than attempt to continuously alter the focus as the aircraft approaches: this can be done, but is difficult to do so successfully with fast-moving jets. I therefore usually pre-focus, and let the depth of field of the lens compensate for any inaccuracy in focussing.

Selection of a film with a fast speed assists. There are several colour slide and colour print films rated at 100 or 200 ASA, with

Detail photographs obtained at air displays such as these shots of a Mirage 2000C at Mildenhall can prove invaluable in detailing a model; depending on the kit manufacturer, some features of the aircraft are reproduced in a greatly simplified form for ease of manufacture.

colour print films also available at 400 ASA, which will enable a fast shutter speed to be used. My personal choice of film is Kodachrome 64, which is renowned for its fine grain and colour rendition. The speed of 64 ASA is perfectly adequate on a good sunny day, and I do not contemplate using any other film. Should the weather conditions be poor, I usually do not bother to take any shots of the flying display at all, unless something special is flying. After 15 years of photography I know that the results I will obtain from shooting on a bad day will be inferior, so I save the film for use on a better day.

However, I cannot expect other photographers to adopt such a philosophical attitude. It must be remembered that, despite the use of a fast film to enable one to shoot on a poor day, the photographs will still be of a poorly lit subject under an overcast sky: in fact, a true rendition of the conditions prevailing when the shutter button was pressed.

MUSEUMS

These locations also present the modeller with a real challenge to take some good photographs during a visit. Museums share many features with air displays, with the common use of crowd barriers preventing close and unhindered access to the exhibits. Any museum curator will gladly explain why such safeguards are necessary—parts of the aircraft go missing otherwise! The greatest problems lie in attempting to photograph the aircraft inside the museum buildings, where it is relatively dark. Some museums prohibit the use of flash or tripods, so it is best to check with the curator prior to a visit if any such restrictions apply, rather than meet them head-on on the day of your visit.

Space is at a premium in all museums, so there is great pressure for them to utilise every possible square inch of it. It is better to pack the exhibits close together, rather than leave one of them outside to the ravages of the British climate. The aircraft are thus quite difficult to photograph if a good overall shot is required, with exhibits having interlocking wings, or being tucked in beneath each other. Photographers may thus be forced to admit defeat in these situations and purchase a photograph (taken in more favourable circumstances!) from the museum shop.

It is often quite possible to photograph inside hangars without the use of a tripod, because of the extensive glazing. This Jet Provost T4 of the CATCS was photographed at RAF Shawbury in September 1983.

AIRFIELDS

Opportunities to photograph aircraft on an operational military or civil airfield are a rare privilege, and should not be abused. Many general aviation airfields are quite open, and it is tempting to simply wander on and take all the photographs you want. Such an idyllic state of affairs may have existed in the 1950s, but today the increasing prevalence of theft and malicious damage has brought such a golden age to an end. If

Some of the best results can be obtained at operational airfields with photographs taken over the fence, such as this Lightning F6 of 11Sqn. at Crash Gate 3, RAF Binbrook.

caught wandering around an airfield, one will be unceremoniously ejected!

The only way to pursue photography (apart from joining the local flying club) is to write and request permission. Remember, however, that these are commercial enterprises and the owners or managers may not be able to spare anyone to conduct an enthusiast around—it is simply not economically viable to do so. It should be possible, however, to photograph quite freely from outside the confines of the airfield: if this involves access onto private land, the permission of the owner should be obtained.

Military airfields are quite a different proposition. With regard to the all-embracing provisions of the Official Secrets Act, the legality of photographing military aircraft from outside a station is open to doubt. Should photographers simply turn up unannounced at a military airfield and start taking photographs through the fence, they must expect to come under the close scrutiny of the security services who will, quite justifiably, want to know who they are and what they are doing! A procedure which I have used in the past is to write to the Community Relations Officer of the station concerned, requesting permission to take photographs of their aircraft outside the boundary of the station; a favourable reply is often received. Some stations strictly forbid the taking of photographs, with warning notices to that effect, and it would be prudent to obey.

Many enlightened stations provide spotter's car parks and enclosures, but in the absence of these it is often possible to find some vantage point where the proceedings may be photographed. Remember to respect the rights of the person upon whose property you are trespassing, and seek permission beforehand wherever this is possible. Care should also be taken not to obstruct the highway with your parked vehicle.

Visits to military airfields can sometimes be arranged, but it must be said that the likelihood of an individual photographer being granted the privilege of such a visit is slight. However do not be deterred, and write to the Community Relations Officer outlining your requirements. The best proposition is to request a visit as part of an organised group, as visits by members of an ATC squadron, aviation society or modelling club are more likely to be accepted. A small number is best, say 12 at the most, and these should preferably be all adults—though a few teenagers would be acceptable. If the request is granted, it will

Lightning, photographed at RAF Binbrook in August 1987.

probably be scheduled for the working week, i.e. between 9.00am and 5.00pm, Monday to Friday.

Badger the secretary of your local modelling club to write requesting a club visit. If you are not a member of such a club—join one! Specifically request permission to take photographs: do not automatically assume that this will be granted. You do not want to learn that photography is not permitted after having driven 100 miles to the airfield.

Once on the tarmac of an operational station, etiquette is of prime importance. Do exactly as instructed by your escort, and be particularly careful about dropping litter or pieces of photographic equipment: a lens cap or film canister ingested into a jet engine would cause thousands of pounds worth of damage, or may endanger a life. Do not take any illicit photographs, after having been told not to! Your conduct on the station will determine whether any such facilities are ever extended to such a group again. One visit by an ill-disciplined rabble will place an embargo on future visits, so please do not foul it up for the rest of us!

Personally, I find photography at operational airfields to be the most satisfying of all. One is often able to examine an aircraft at leisure and obtain some good detail photographs, and to compose a pleasing photograph of the complete aircraft without the detrimental influences of crowds of people and barriers in the shot. Even outside airfields one can usually take good quality general views of aircraft on the taxiway or on approach.

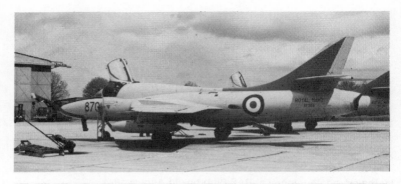

My favourite place to photograph aircraft is in their natural environment:
the flightline of an operational airfield.

COMMERCIAL SOURCES

However good a photographer you may be, your own resources will be inadequate to support the research needs of
modelling, unless a limited choice of subject is acceptable. The
fact has to be faced that I cannot visit RAF Wattisham to
procure photographs of 29 Sqn. Lightnings any more: similarly,
whilst the 3rd TFW still fly F-4Es, a trip to Clark AFB in the
Philippines is beyond my resources! Recourse must therefore
be made to other reference sources, and, once again,
modellers of today have access to an incredibly wide field of
information...

Aviation photo libraries

There are several such enterprises which regularly advertise in
the pages of the aviation and modelling press; copy colour

slides and both colour and black and white prints are available. Typically, a monthly list will be issued, backed up by seperate catalogues listing all the photographs available of a specific type.

Less well known is the fact that both the RAF Museum and the Imperial War Museum open their photographic files for research purposes; visits must be made in person, by appointment only. On a less formal basis, several organisations provide original colour slides on approval; again, these services will be found advertised in the aviation press.

Books

There is an absolute wealth of reference sources available to the modeller in book form, this field of publishing having mushroomed over the past 10 years. It would be invidious to mention any particular publications by name, but there are several ranges of books aimed specifically at the modeller and which will be of great interest: these are the *in detail & scale* series from the USA, the *Aeroguide* series and the *Aircraft Archive* series; there are also hundreds of other publications aimed at the enthusiast market which modellers will find equally useful.

Availability of such specialist titles in the local bookshop may not prove adequate, but there are numerous mail order companies who specialise in such literature clamouring for your business. Write to one and request a copy of their catalogue: the range of titles available, many of them from overseas, will astonish you.

Several of these companies also attend air displays and the larger modelling events such as the IPMS Nationals at Stoneleigh each November, where you may have a good opportunity to browse through their stock. One such company which I regularly use myself is **Midland Counties Publications**, 24 The Hollow, Earl Shilton, Leicester LE9 7NA; you will find many others in the advertisement sections of the aviation and modelling press who provide a similar service.

Magazines

The shelves of major high street newsagents groan under the weight of magazines devoted to modelling and associated aviation subjects. A good example of a modelling title is *Scale Models International* which includes regular articles on aircraft modelling and provides reference material in the form of

One of the joys of visiting military airfields is the chance of seeing something out of the ordinary: almost anything can turn up. Pictured here are a Mirage F1C of EC30 on the Binbrook flightline in August 1987 whilst on a squadron exchange visit, and a Canberra B6 of the RAE Bedford seen at RAF Wyton in June 1987.

photographs, and artwork, on a wide range of subjects. In addition to *SMI* and similar modelling magazines, there are many magazines published each month on various aspects of aviation which will provide first class reference material for modellers. Several also include a regular modelling column.

Many aviation magazines are published in Europe and elsewhere in the world, and these are often available from the specialist aviation booksellers referred to earlier.

COLLATION OF REFERENCES

For reference sources to be of any use to the modeller, he must be aware that he has the reference in the first place. After a few years of gathering reference material it becomes necessary to devise some system of cataloguing the information that has been obtained, so that it may be referred to in the future.

My personal collection of colour transparencies totals some 13,000 slides, and the collection grows at about 1,000 each year. After a few years' photography I still had a pretty good idea of what was in the collection, but this soon grew too big for my brain capacity! I now allocate a reference number to each slide taken, which is entered in several hardback exercise books in numerical order. By scanning through its pages, I can see what photographs I took on any particular expedition.

Backing up this strictly numerical sequence, a loose leaf folder is kept wherein I cross reference the slides in type order. Some of my colleagues have adopted this subjective approach as their sole record, allocating sequences of numbers with an identifying prefix, e.g. LN or PH for photographs of Lightnings and Phantoms respectively. After spending a few winter's evenings cross-indexing my slides, I sometimes wish I had adopted that system to begin with!

Consideration has been given to storing this information on a micro-computer, and I have seen several advertisements in the aviation press for computer programmes specifically designed for the filing of aircraft photographs. However, when I consider how many rolls of Kodachrome that I could buy for the same cost as a micro-computer, disc drive and monitor, I begin to appreciate the merits of my paper-based system.

Another peculiarity of mine is that I still take black and white photographs. These bring their own storage and retrieval problems with them. My personal preference is to have the film developed and a contact print taken of the strips of negatives. The contact sheets are filed away in a lever-arch binder, annotated as to the date and place where taken. The contact sheet may be examined at leisure, and only those prints which are required are printed. I store the negatives in a few old Frog kit boxes (the *Orange* series are ideal), the negative wallet being identified by a sticker showing the date and location. The reason I still use black and white film is because one can shoot a large number of detail shots relatively inexpensively, as only those negatives which are required are printed.

Modellers will soon find it necessary to catalogue their printed sources of reference. I am sure that I am not alone in having spent all night rummaging through my back issues of magazines trying to find one particular article or photograph. It only seemed like last year when I saw it—but it usually turns out to have been published five years previously. To prevent myself wasting too many evenings in fruitless searches for magazine articles, I decided to catalogue these sources of reference also.

The ubiquitous loose-leaf binder comes into its own again: I simply allocate a page to each aircraft type, and then list thereon relevant articles to be found in my stock of magazines. I use a simple code to refer to each magazine: 'AI' for *Aircraft Illustrated*, 'SM' for *Scale Models International*, and so on. Show the year and month of the issue, and put down brief details of what is contained within the article. An example of such a note would be:

"AP 3/71 – 29 Sqn. at RAF Wattisham, F3"

Entered on the Lightning page, this would direct me to the *March 1971* issue of *Air Pictorial* for an article on the F3s of 29 Sqn. at RAF Wattisham. The compilation of such information will take some considerable time at the outset but, once established, it is easily kept up to date. Hopefully, no more modelling time will be wasted looking for references.

I sincerely hope that modellers who are interested in compiling their own sources of reference will find the content of this chapter to be of some use to them. I cannot claim any great expertise in the field of photography, but I think I have learned enough from 15 years of photographing military aircraft to enable me to obtain passable results. Perhaps my greatest failing is in being ready to throw in the towel when conditions become adverse; many other photographers may be getting acceptable results after I have packed up and gone home! However, I set my own standards from having thrown away boxes of slides in the past when shooting in such conditions: unless I can get a good result, I tend not to bother at all. This may be somewhat selective, but it is also much cheaper—the film can always be used on a better day.

In its most basic form, almost any photograph will have some use as a source of reference. However, I am only happy when I can be proud of the resulting photograph, and not feel ashamed should it appear in print with my name credited against it. Aesthetic values have therefore overridden the content of the photograph in purely reference terms. I want to take more than simply a reference photograph, but I cannot expect everyone else to share my views.

A word of warning: modellers may find aircraft photography so interesting that they completely abandon kit-bashing in favour of chasing about the country after aircraft. This happened to me: it could happen to you!

SOME USEFUL ADDRESSES

MUSEUMS

1. The Royal Air Force
   Museum,
   Hendon,
   London NW9 5LL.

2. The Imperial War Museum,
   Lambeth Road,
   London SE1 6HZ.

3. The Fleet Air Arm Museum,
   RNAS Yeovilton,
   Somerset BA22 8HT.

AVIATION PHOTO LIBRARIES

1. Military Aircraft
   Photographs,
   East Cliff,
   Stotfield Road,
   Lossiemouth,
   Moray,
   Scotland IV31 6QT.

2. Aviation Photo News,
   56 Tachbrook Road,
   Feltham,
   Middlesex TW14 9PB.

3. Mil Slides,
   106 Selsdon Road,
   South Croydon,
   Surrey CR2 6PF.

MAIL ORDER BOOKSELLERS

1. Midland Counties
   Publications,
   24 The Hollow,
   Earl Shilton,
   Leicester LE9 7NA.

2. Beaumont Aviation
   Literature,
   656 Holloway Road,
   London N19 3PD.

5   VACFORM BUILDING

GEOFF PRENTICE

Vacform building is not for beginners. Having said that, vacform models are not half as difficult to make as many people like to think they are. As a bonus, they offer a lot of subjects that you are not going to see from any other source plus an outlet for all your frustrated craftsmanship.

Before attempting your first vacform it is necessary to get a good few conventional kits under your belt so that you have mastered all the basic techniques like gluing and seam filling. The trouble is, that will make you a practiced modeller who is used to succeeding and it may come a little hard when you encounter the initial failures and frustrations associated with vacforms. All too many people fall at this first hurdle and tell themselves that if they, as experienced modellers, cannot make vacforms then they must be very difficult indeed. I must confess that I fell into that category myself initially and gave up after the first three or four total failures. I was cured by the release of a vacform subject that I just had to build so I pressed on and overcame the difficulties. In the process, my whole attitude to modelling changed; I found the satisfaction of winning through against the difficulties so great that I became a vacform addict. Enough of this talk of failure and difficulty— let's have a look at the beast...

WHAT IS A VACFORM?

I once heard an experienced, and much respected, modeller refer to vacforms as 100% flash. This was in the early days and you would be right in thinking that he was not too enthusiastic about the new medium. The basis for his comment was that all the parts are formed on a carrier sheet and you have to cut them out and prepare them before you have anything that resembles a conventional kit.

This method of production has its roots in the packaging industry. Indeed one of the fathers of the vacform says that he got the idea while looking at the moulded plastic tray inside his

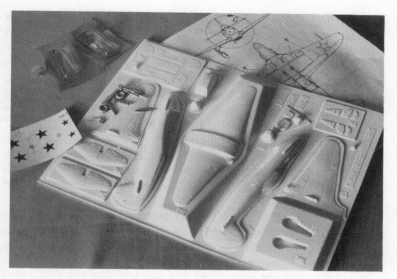

A typical good quality modern vacform kit and the finished article. JMGT's Yak 3 in 1:48 scale.

wife's chocolate box. The beauty of vacforms is that kits can be produced fairly cheaply from basic materials and are able to recover their production costs over relatively short production runs unlike conventional kits that require machine tools costing many tens of thousands of pounds.

In their simplest form, vacforms are made by drawing heat-softened plastic sheet onto a master carving of the subject's parts and allowing it to cool. This is the basic male moulding process and is still used by some of the smaller producers. The parts so produced are often not well defined and all attempts at moulding detail on the parts results in the best detail being found on the inside of the parts, while that on the outside is rounded and indistinct. From that basic method, the producers have evolved a system of producing a more durable female mould which permits the creation of sharply-defined parts with crisp surface detail. The method by which this is done is unimportant to the modeller, but he should learn to distinguish between the products of the two methods as this will help him assess the kits on offer.

In general, male moulded kits will be more demanding to build than females though there are a few more sophisticated products that used a mixture of the two techniques to good effect. Aside from the basic chore of cutting out, the other drawback of the medium is that the vacform process is not well suited to the production of small, highly detailed items like undercarriages or complex shapes like propellers. Many kits attempt to supply the modeller with these parts, sometimes to good effect, but the quality rarely, if ever, matches that of conventional moulding in plastic or other mediums.

In recent years this has led to the introduction of 'multi-media' kits featuring vacform airframes with detail parts produced in another material. At least one range of models is now using resin casting, white metal and photo-etched brass to support the vacform parts in its kits. Armed with such a kit and basic vacform construction skills, the modeller is in as good a position to build a first-rate replica as the purchaser of a conventional 'super-kit'.

Kit selection
Since there are very few examples of duplication of subjects in the same scale in the vacform world, the prospective purchaser is unlikely to be faced with a wide choice of kits of his chosen subject. However, if he is a newcomer to vacforms there are a few things that he should bear in mind. First, although standards are generally improving, there is not the uniformity of quality in vacforms that is found in conventional kits. Some are highly-developed products which supply virtually everything you will need while others are basic, undetailed shapes that require the builder to scratch build all the small parts and provide all the surface detail himself. Sadly, it must also be said that there are still a few kits around which are simply rubbish.

As many vacform kits are sold by mail order it is not always possible to inspect them before you buy. Seek advice from other modellers, if possible, and read magazine reviews. Even if the particular subject that interests you is not being discussed, it should be possible to get an idea of the kind of kit produced by any particular manufacturer. (If you do find that you have purchased something which is inappropriate to your needs, or beyond your level of competence, you will find that most mail order suppliers will be understanding if you return the goods undamaged).

Subject choice for your first vacform is crucial. You want something that you are likely to be able to build without too much trouble. Avoid bi-planes and propellers unless they are supplied in another medium. Larger scales can also present problems since they will demand more detailing work and you may not be ready for that just yet. Look for a kit that supplies essential small parts in metal, resin or injection moulding and, above all, seek a subject for which you have sufficient enthusiasm to carry you through a few difficulties.

Preparation

Having made your choice, read the instructions (which may range from a substantial booklet via a three-view drawing to nothing at all!) and set about identifying the various parts and the construction method. Take the vacform sheet(s) and hold it up to a strong light. This will enable you to see where the plastic has been stretched most and the walls of the parts are thinnest. Wherever really thin places are evident, fill the rear of the thin area with a non-aggressive filler (Milliput or similar) to support the weak spot. With experience you will learn that this is only essential in those places which are likely to be stressed or worked on later in construction but initially it's best to take no chances.

Sometimes the thin parts will already have been crushed in transit. In most cases it is possible to push the damaged area back into shape from the inside. Try to use something rounded and as near the desired shape as possible to do this, and avoid excessive force at all costs. The end of a paintbrush is ideal in most cases but remember, the plastic is likely to be very thin. Wherever possible, support the repaired area from the inside with filler and, if damage remains on the outside surface, coat that with filler too and allow to dry before sanding the part back to shape.

Once you are satisfied with the integrity of the parts, it is time to consider cutting them out. There are many different ways of approaching this task and your technique will undoubtably change with experience. Many modellers like to provide themselves with a reference point for sanding at this stage. There are two popular methods, both of which are effective. You can run a sharp pencil around the part at the junction between it and the carrier sheet before you cut it out, or you can spray the whole part a neutral grey shade and let it dry before cutting out. The object of both methods is to give a clear demarcation line between the part itself and the excess plastic at its base which must be removed by sanding. Few experienced builders bother with either, since to the practiced eye, the edge of the part is plain to see, but in the early days it is a useful safeguard.

Removing the parts may be undertaken in a variety of ways and each will affect the amount of sanding that will have to be done. The safest method, though one that will result in the longest sanding job, is to cut around the part about 1/8 in. away from its edge, thus leaving a margin of spare plastic around it. The quickest method is simply to flex the plastic away from the junction between the part and the sheet until it snaps. This only works on larger, deeply drawn parts with any degree of certainty and should never be done if the plastic is thin or the edges of the parts are ill-defined. This method results in a significant reduction in the amount of plastic which has to be sanded away, as does cutting vertically around the parts with a sharp knife. The most advanced and time-saving method is to score at as shallow an angle as possible around the parts before snapping the plastic away. A very sharp knife and a steady hand is required for this method and I would not commend it to the inexperienced as it holds danger for both the parts and your fingers!

There are no rights and wrongs about cutting out and the majority of builders use a combination of all the methods on a single model. Experience will tell you which parts are best suited to which process and also, the likely reaction of the plastic in any given kit to each. Until you have gained the confidence to want to experiment, my advice is to err on the side of caution because a little extra sanding is preferable to a ruined kit.

Opinions vary about how much of a kit should be cut out at one time. Some modellers like to cut all the major parts out at the beginning. I, on the other hand, prefer only to remove them as they are required, since the sheet gives them some protection and makes them easier to find when they are needed. Once again, there is no hard and fast rule, but what is essential is that you do not start sanding any part until you have cut out any others in the same structural group. It is all too easy to sand half a fuselage and then discover that it won't match its mate which is still on the sheet. Radial engine cowlings that fit

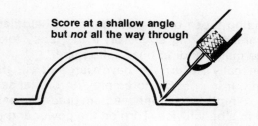

Score at a shallow angle but *not* all the way through

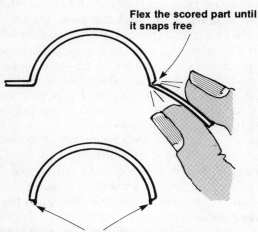

Flex the scored part until it snaps free

This method minimises the need for sanding— only the shaded area has to be removed

on the front of fuselages must always be cut out at the same time as the fuselage halves, so that they can be used as references during sanding.

Sanding

Undoubtably the dullest, yet most critical, aspect of vacform building, this process will decide whether your project will succeed or fail. The essential thing to remember is that it is a lot easier to remove material than it is to put it back, so proceed with caution!

The basic sanding tool is a piece of wet and dry paper (320 grade or coarser) taped to a flat surface, 1/4 in. plate glass is ideal. Ensure that one edge of the paper coincides with the edge of the sanding board as this will enable you to sand tighter corners and also to sand one area of a part at a time. The second essential is a sanding block, either one of the DIY shop's foam blocks or a strip of wet and dry taped to a balsa block, or strip of wood. This will be used for tidying up local areas, sanding those parts that cannot be held flat against a board, thinning trailing edges or, if the fancy takes you, to replace the main sanding board altogether.

If you are really in a hurry, or have a large kit with thick plastic to deal with, it is possible to employ an orbital sander quite effectively. Simply load it with medium grade paper and clamp it inverted in a bench vice. Turn on the power and you have a vibrating sanding table that will only have any effect when you press a part against it. Release the pressure and the part will simply move about with the tool and no sanding will take place. A mask and goggles are desirable as you are obliged to work dry. You must work in short bursts as too long an application tends to melt the plastic. It sounds rather hectic but, with a little practice, it can be a real time saver. The largest vacform I ever built was sanded inside an hour by this method. Not for beginners or delicate kits however!

Commence manual sanding by holding the part flat against the paper and working it in a circular motion. This helps to ensure that the plastic is being removed evenly. Go slowly at first and move your fingers around on the part to make certain that you don't apply prolonged pressure to any particular area. If you have a datum line work almost up to it then set the piece aside and bring its partner up to the same stage. While sanding the second piece compare it frequently with the first. The vacforming process can result in parts that do not match

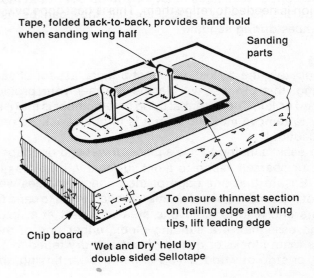

Tape, folded back-to-back, provides hand hold when sanding wing half

Sanding parts

To ensure thinnest section on trailing edge and wing tips, lift leading edge

Chip board

'Wet and Dry' held by double sided Sellotape

exactly so you need to allow a margin for error. On occasions, it may be necessary to sand parts slightly more, or slightly less, to achieve a good fit.

When you are satisfied that you have a good match, finish off both halves either on the sanding board or with a block remembering to check for fit frequently. If you have cut the parts out with a margin of spare material around them then, as you reach the edge of the part, you will find that a tell-tale sliver of plastic curls away from the part; at this stage *stop sanding*.

There are some surprisingly strongly held opinions about whether sanding should be carried out wet or dry. Having tried both I find little to choose between them, except that one produces clouds of dust while the other leaves you with a messy sludge and tends to make the paper rise off the board. I do not propose to engage in the debate here; I work dry most of the time but can see no objection to the other method if that is your preference. The majority of parts can be hand held while sanding but the smaller or flatter items (wings, tailplane halves etc.) may require handles to improve your purchase on them. These are generally made by sticking loops of masking tape to the parts but I find, that in some circumstances, blobs of Blu-Tack are preferable and longer lasting.

Wings and tail surfaces present their own particular problems during the sanding phase. The vacform process causes all trailing edges to be moulded too thick (otherwise they would not stand proud of the backing sheet) so extra attention is needed to refine them. This is best done by use of a

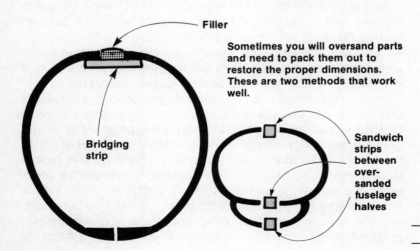

Filler

Bridging strip

Sometimes you will oversand parts and need to pack them out to restore the proper dimensions. These are two methods that work well.

Sandwich strips between over-sanded fuselage halves

sanding block drawing it along the inside of the wing half to produce a knife like edge to the part. Some preparatory work can be done with a scalpel drawn spanwise along the wing with the blade trailing; this will remove thin curls of plastic and is useful for reducing thick plastic quickly. Many small biplane kits feature single-surface wings and tails and, having sanded the parts down to the datum line, it is necessary to round off the leading edges and to taper the trailing edges into the undersurface contours to create a smooth aerofoil section.

The wings of subjects with di or anhedral often have either their upper or lower wing sections moulded full span. This assists in construction as it results in built-in angles but calls for caution while sanding. It becomes vital to sand the part in two, or three, operations making use of the edge of the sanding board. Where the centre section is moulded in the bottom half of a wing with dihedral it is necessary to sand its edges with a sanding block. All sanding should be done before attempting to remove cockpit, wheelwell or intake areas as you want the parts to be as strong as possible during the process.

Bulkheads and spars

Unlike conventional kits vacform parts are fairly flexible and, since their mating surfaces are slim, joints are prone to failure unless the larger structures and load points are supported internaly. All the best kits include the vital bulkheads, either as moulded parts or by means of templates, but in some cases you will have to plan and design your own. Small models require little more than that needed to blank off the cockpit area or to prevent 'see through' but larger subjects will need support around the wing root area and at intervals along the fuselage. As you will almost certainly be handling your model by its wings and there are no tabs to support the root joint, a simple mainspar is also a wise addition on larger subjects.

Plotting the shape of a curved fuselage interior is a thankless task unless you invest in a simple gauge. These can be found in DIY stores and are intended to plot the shape of tile or carpet cuts around difficult areas. They consist of a number of plates held in a handle in a comb-like manner. Each plate is free to slide relative to its neighbour so that when you press the comb against a shape the plates record its contours. It is a simple matter to transfer the shape onto plastic sheet thus establishing the bulkhead profile. Wing spars are a much simpler proposition as they can be drawn directly from a head on

(Above) Internal work is vital: this XB-42 has had simple vertical spacers fitted to prevent the shells from flexing. This kit is unusual in that the wings slide into fuselage cut-outs. A wing spar is still valuable. (Below) With all the internal bracing the parts are quite robust and the model slips together accurately with the wing spar providing the key. Note the strips glued along the joint line at stress points.

drawing of the subject assuming you have one. Don't forget to make allowance for the thickness of the wing shells however. In most cases, it is only necessary to extend the spar out about $\frac{1}{4}$ span from the root.

There is an alternative to bulkheads and that is to fill the fuselage halves with foam. This can be purchased from specialist model shops and comes as a two-part mixture. Once combined the fluids froth up and will fill any cavity you pour the mix into. After a few minutes a crisp, aerated biscuit-like substance has formed and set hard. Excess can be trimmed with an hacksaw blade. The cured foam can be drilled and cut at will and may be sanded and glued quite simply. The chemicals involved do demand careful handling in their liquid state, but once cured, the foam is pleasant and safe to work with. Parts filled in this manner are very robust and it is easy to make well-supported cockpit and wheelwell interiors. I am told that in some climates the foam may expand if subjected to temperature rises and this has disastrous effects on joints but, as I have never experienced this phenomenon, I cannot comment further.

Construction

You may have been wondering when we would get around to this! In fact, it differs very little from conventional kit assembly once you have done all the preparation. However, the thinness of the walls of the parts, and the absence of location pegs can be a problem on large parts, so a little more support is required. This takes the form of strips glued along one fuselage half to form a lip over which the other half locates. The strips also provide support for any filler that may be needed. If the fuselage section along the joint line is fairly flat, then the strips can be longitudinal only breaking to miss bulkheads and cut-outs. If it is curved, it is preferable to use a number of strips glued across the joint line so that they will flex as the two halves are joined thus assuming the internal shape of the mating half. Naturally, to achieve this effect, it is advisable to use thin, pliable plastic for the lip and not to attempt too great an overlap.

Once the bulkheads and the lips are in place, tape the halves together and rough out any cockpit, wheelwell or other openings that are needed. Do not place too much reliance on moulded lines purporting to represent the extent of the cut-outs. It is quite common for these to match neither each other, nor the dimensions of any internal structures. Make constant reference to any internal parts and clean out the rough holes with the two halves mated so that they match each other. When making cockpit cut-outs use any canopy parts as a guide to ensure they will fit over the hole.

Never use tube cement on vacforms, always opt for one of the liquids. The techniques are exactly as detailed in the chapter on the construction of conventional kits, except that even more emphasis must be placed on accurate alignment of parts before applying the liquid. Also, it is sometimes beneficial to tape together difficult joints and to allow capillary action to carry the adhesive under the tape. When you do that, give ample time for the joint to harden before removing the tape and run a little extra liquid along the joint afterwards to eliminate any gaps.

Having done all the right things you should have arrived at a basic airframe which looks like a poorly made injection kit. That is not your fault, or that of the kit, it is simply in the nature of vacforms that seam lines are a little less regular and there is the odd gap or divot to be dealt with. There is no cause to despair, you simply apply the seam and gap erradication techniques that you have learned in the past and you will soon have something quite presentable. I find that gaps are best treated with Milliput, filling them first with little rolls of the putty as mixed then smoothing it over with a wet finger or knife blade. The most likely location of gaps are around the wing roots where anything except a butt joint seems to create problems

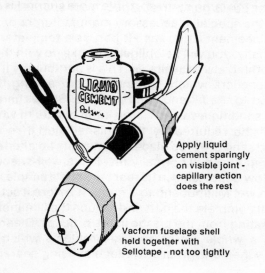

Apply liquid
cement sparingly
on visible joint -
capillary action
does the rest

Vacform fuselage shell
held together with
Sellotape - not too tightly

103

Filling is a critical part of vacform building. This Falcon Sea Hawk has had a great deal of Milliput expended on the joint between the front and rear fuselage sections.

for the kit producers. The wet working method is particularly valuable here as it simplifies the creation of smooth fillets.

Having dealt with the large parts you then have to come to terms with the smaller items. These are less of a chore with many modern kits than they used to because they are quite often supplied in another medium. However, there are still many kits on sale that feature tiny moulded items that you are advised to fill before removing from the sheet then sand to shape. In 99% of cases this advice is pure fantasy because the method simply will not work for something the size of a 1:72 scale step or Lewis gun barrel. Check your spares box, look at the lists of the specialist accessory manufacturers or scratch-build a replacement using the kit part as a template.

Occasionally, you will be obliged to make do with the kit part because nothing else is available. This is particularly true in the case of propellers which, fortunately, are among the parts better suited to the fill and sand process. Since there is little purpose in sanding away at a large lump of filler of which only 10–15% will be required by the finished part I reverse the process and sand the prop blade to as near its finished shape as possible first. That will normally result in a well-shaped blade with a shallow depression in its rear face. It is a simple matter to fill this with wet Milliput and to smooth it before it sets. A final sanding will complete the part and reduce the likelihood of the putty separating from the plastic in the process. Clear vacform parts have a whole set of special problems which tend to overshadow their one great advantage of being nearer to scale

Vacform biplanes are not as difficult as many people think. The struts of this D.H.5 were cut from Contrail aerofoil material and allowed to dry before attempting to mount the top wing. A simple paper jig was made from the plan to assist in aligning the wings.

thickness than any injection moulded equivalent. The material from which they are formed does not react to glue in the normal way. It also tends to be much harder than the white plastic and is more difficult to sand and shape. Small scissors are best for cutting out canopies but then I am afraid there is little choice but to go through the tedious process of sanding and test fitting before fixing them in place with white glue. Some kits give you solid mouldings of canopy shapes which are useful as templates. Cut them out and make them fit the canopy opening; having achieved a reasonable fit, place the clear part over the top and trim it as near to the size of the solid one as possible. Failing all else you can normally get the windscreen to fit and it is possible to camouflage the poor fit of the remainder by mounting it in an open position. That does have the drawback that you have to detail the cockpit interior of course!

Flat windows are normally best replaced with another material. Good quality white glue can be used to skin them over and will dry clear, Carr's make an acetate product that can also be used to good effect. Clear plastic sheet and even thin glass can be cut to shape by scribing with a sharp point and snapping away the excess. A template is essential for this work and either the Verlinden Productions product (recommended for all rescribing work) or standard draughtsman's templates may be used. Ultra-thin glass can be obtained from scientific suppliers in the form of microscope slide covers and, although it can only be used for flat panels, it is surprisingly easy to work with and very realistic.

Modifications and Improvements

All the same conversions and improvements that can be done with conventional kits can be undertaken with vacforms. In many cases the work is more straightforward as the thin walled parts are much easier to cut and, any sections which are removed for open panels and the like, are near to scale thickness. The experience gained in making vacforms will stand the modeller in good stead and give him confidence to try quite complex adaptations.

The vacform modeller will need to provide himself with stocks of plastic sheet in various thicknesses, plastic strip and tubes and rods in both plastic and metal. With these basics, plus the host of specialist supplies of white metal and photo-etched parts now available, there is no limit to the detailing that can be attempted. Start with something fairly simple like boxing in and detailing wheelwells. Assemble the wing halves then cut strips of 10 thou. sheet. Glue these vertically between the edges of the wheelwell sides and the upper wing. Run liquid glue around the joins and when dry trim off the excess on the undersurface. Even if you don't have accurate details of the prototype, glue a few strips chordwise across the roof of the well to represent stiffeners and add some thin rod, wire or stretched sprue around the sides of the wells. Once painted, these will give a suitably 'busy' appearance to the wells.

Internal detail does not have to be complex to be effective. Contrail rod gives a good impression of the structure while the instrument panels are made by sandwiching clear sheet between two solid layers one of which has been drilled out for the instrument bezels. Etched metal bezels would also have been effective.

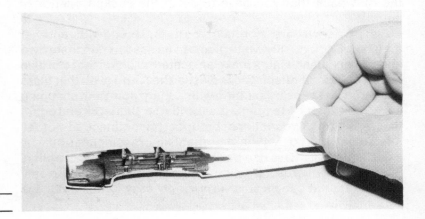

Biplane cockpits will also benefit from strips mounted to indicate the exposed internal structure and a simple instrument panel can be made from thin wood veneer varnished and adorned with a *few* etched brass instrument bezels. Vacform jet kits tend to supply the conventional cockpit bathtub so it is simply a matter of adding some details. If you don't have accurate references (a common problem given the obscure types often modelled in vacform) study pictures of cockpits of similar types from the same era to get a feel for the style of layout. Using either metal bezels or slivers cut from plastic tube lay out the details and wash the whole area with liquid glue. Paint the panel and the instruments as necessary and, when dry, scratch the instrument details inside the bezels with a pin. The white plastic revealed in this way is all that is needed apart from a drop of clear wax or varnish to 'glaze' the instruments.

The ability to stretch sprue is vital to the vacform builder so if you haven't acquired it earlier in your career then do so now. Take a section of smooth sprue or plastic rod and hold it about $1/2$ in. above the tip of a candle flame. Rotate it slowly to give an even application of heat and when it either sags, or starts to swell, remove it from the heat. For thin sprue pull the two ends apart; not too fast or the plastic will break nor too slow which will allow it to harden and will result in shorter, thicker sprue. The longer you wait after removing the sprue from the heat the thicker will be the stretched material.

Sprue has many merits as a modelling aid. It is free and can be found in a great variety of colours so that painting items like rigging and aerials can be avoided. It can be glued with liquid cement and also formed into any cross-section simply by filing the desired shape into the sprue stock before heating. (Aerofoil section rod is particularly useful when stretched as it can be used for thin struts and even for streamlined rigging wires!) Finally, it can be formed into useful shapes while hot. To do this simply wind the plastic around something of the desired shape

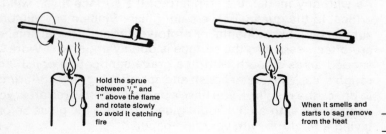

Hold the sprue between $1/2$" and 1" above the flame and rotate slowly to avoid it catching fire

When it smells and starts to sag remove from the heat

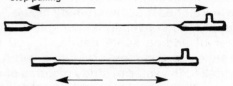

For fine filament pull at once with a steady, even pull. It is quite possible to pull 10ft or more in one go with practice. As soon as resistance is felt, stop pulling

Thicker rods can be made by allowing the sprue to cool for a few moments before pulling and by pulling more slowly

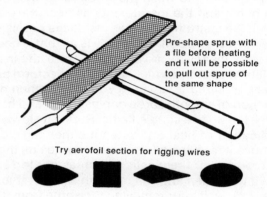

Pre-shape sprue with a file before heating and it will be possible to pull out sprue of the same shape

Try aerofoil section for rigging wires

as you stretch it. Small files and paintbrushes are particularly useful for this purpose and coiled sprue makes perfect DF loops, joystick handles, step stirrups etc.

Sprue stretching is not a difficult technique to learn and once you have the knack you will find endless uses for the product. You will find that sprues from different sources have different properties, even colour can make a difference. Make a collection of the types and colours that you find most useful.

Finishing
As with any model, the standard of the surface finish will be critical to the quality of the paint finish. Since many vacform subjects are experimental or prototype aircraft, metal finishes are often needed so the surface is doubly important. Work all sanded areas smooth with fine grade sandpaper, polish any rough areas with metal polish and spray with grey auto-primer to check the results. If you have a particularly scarred area, you can paint it with a mild liquid glue to restore the gloss before giving a final rub with very fine paper.

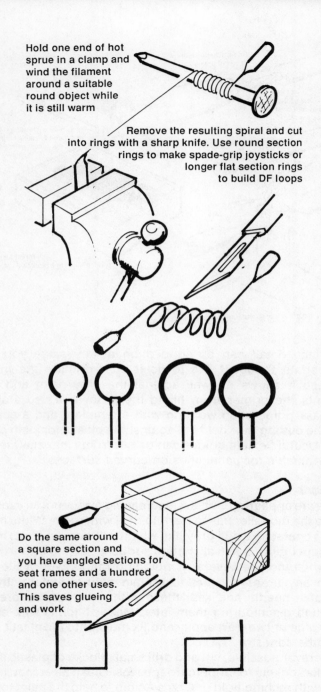

Hold one end of hot sprue in a clamp and wind the filament around a suitable round object while it is still warm

Remove the resulting spiral and cut into rings with a sharp knife. Use round section rings to make spade-grip joysticks or longer flat section rings to build DF loops

Do the same around a square section and you have angled sections for seat frames and a hundred and one other uses. This saves glueing and work

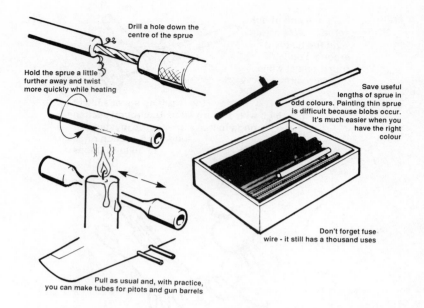

Drill a hole down the centre of the sprue

Hold the sprue a little further away and twist more quickly while heating

Save useful lengths of sprue in odd colours. Painting thin sprue is difficult because blobs occur. It's much easier when you have the right colour

Don't forget fuse wire - it still has a thousand uses

Pull as usual and, with practice, you can make tubes for pitots and gun barrels

Surface detail can be scribed on at any stage you find appropriate though I like to do it after priming the model because it shows up well against the grey paint and also prevents the primer from filling the grooves. I use a sharp compass point when working with a template and a scalpel with the cutting face held flat against the plastic for main panel lines. Useful flexible guides can be cut from clear acetate and are invaluable for panel lines on curved surfaces.

Metal parts

These are appearing with ever increasing frequency in vacform kits so the modeller has to learn to deal with them. White metal comes coated in a dull grey film which will weaken joints made with super glue. Clean all mating surfaces back to bright metal before gluing. Remove any moulding marks with a file and polish any areas that are to remain natural metal with the side of a needle and seal these with clear wax to prevent oxidation discolouring them later. Make all joints with either super glue or two-part epoxy and fix them onto the plastic with the same adhesive.

Wherever possible, cut and drill small blocks of plastic sheet to make sockets for undercarriage legs. Clean all etched metal parts with etching fluid or Carr's Acidip to help the paint to key.

The finished Sea Hawk proves the work was worthwhile: note the use of the open cockpit dodge to overcome difficulties with the fit of the rear section.

I spray all metal parts with grey auto-primer before attempting to paint them (don't forget to mask the natural metal areas).

Conclusion

There is much more to be said about vacform model building because you learn with every model you complete. Not everyone will have the determination to stick with it long enough to master the basics, but those who do persevere, will find that they have expanded their hobby enormously. You will learn much about the nature and capabilities of plastic and will soon find that you can tell how a piece will behave simply by handling it. It will certainly alter the way you look at kits and I doubt you will ever again open a conventional kit without wondering how you can modify or improve it.

6 DIORAMAS

GRAHAM DIXEY

The diorama offers the modeller the scope to extend his activities into a wider field of modelling, as well as allowing him to display the result of his workmanship to much better effect. This applies to any fields of modelling and not just to those involving military figures and vehicles. What then is a 'diorama'?

Our normal concept of a diorama is quite different from the *Concise Oxford Dictionary*'s definition. Paraphrasing somewhat, 'a diorama is a spectacular painting which produces natural effects, sunrise for example, by the direction and colour of light falling upon it'. No mention of modelling at all! Thus the word has been borrowed and its meaning modified to suit our own purposes.

In these terms, then, a diorama represents a scene, created from a number of figures and/or other items, natural or man-

Note the devotion to detail in this diorama by John Hunter. The wall is made by plastering over a core of expanded polystyrene, cutting in the detail. Wooden parts are made from balsawood. Most modellers make the mistake of understating the amount of debris present, but not this one!

There is a great variety of plastic kits, that not only provide the supporting accessories, but may also be used as the nucleus for a vignette or diorama.

made, such as trees, vehicles, aeroplanes, ships, etc, displayed on some form of modelled groundwork. Effectively it is a three-dimensional 'frozen moment in time'. It is this that gives it its special appeal.

Sources and composition

Every diorama is based upon some particular idea. The question is, where does this idea come from? Apart from inspiration itself, what other sources are there? There are many possible sources—there are paintings, either in books or museums, and there are photographs. The two World Wars and the Vietnam war are popular subjects with modellers and all three have been extensively photographed. The fact is that, whatever the period of the modeller's interest, visual references can be found somewhere.

However, there is another, easily accessible source that the modeller might like to consider and that is a kit. There is a very good selection of kits that contain the ingredients of a diorama.

In plastic kits containing figures there is a great variety in the sizes from 25 mm to 54 mm, or the alternative 1:35 scale. A brief look at current makers' catalogues reveals that there is much to be had especially for the Napoleonic and WW2 periods. There is even a range of 'diorama kits' produced by the Italian maker ESCI, 28 altogether, of which 27 are for WW2 and the other for the Vietnam War. But for those modellers able to form mental pictures of what they would like to model, many splendid dioramas can be created from existing figure and vehicle kits, of which there is a vast range from a number of well-known makers. It is, of course, equally possible to create dioramas with ships (e.g. harbour scenes), or with aircraft and perhaps some figures or just ancilliary items, or even with car kits and figures of the appropriate scale.

Composition is a thorny subject, and there is no space here for a detailed discussion. Suffice it to say that the arrangement of pieces in the diorama will affect the impact of the scene. If part of a painting, or a photograph, is being copied into model form, the layout is largely predetermined, though unlike the source, the diorama can be viewed from various angles. It is always a good idea to experiment with the arrangement of pieces on a board, perhaps the actual base, before committing them to the final model. When it looks right and each figure, vehicle or whatever, seems to be related to everything else in the scene in a natural way, then the composition is probably sound enough. The tendency to clutter up the scene with items that have little real relation to what is going on should be resisted. Before half-burying a waggon wheel, helmet or jerry-can in the groundwork, the modeller should ask himself why it is there and how it got there.

Groundwork
The nature of the groundwork can be extremely varied. It may be flat, hilly, grassy, muddy, rocky, sandy or bare earth—or various combinations of these. It may be a cobbled road surface, or plain tarmacadam. It may not even be solid at all but be part of a river, lake or the open sea! In an interior scene it may consist of a wooden, tiled or stone flagged floor. Needless to say, to be effective it has to be done well. I will now describe some of the ways in which these surfaces can be represented.

The basic groundwork is usually produced using some form of modelling plaster. Examples are Tetrion, plaster of Paris and Carr's 'Topsoil'. The latter is produced especially for modellers and has some unusual characteristics, one of which is the length of time that it takes to dry, which is substantial; however, this does allow the surface to be textured in various ways while it is still in a workable state. The problem with some plasters is the shrinkage and cracking that occurs when they dry out. Those mentioned above are reasonably free from this defect, especially if they are applied in thin layers only. Any attempt to produce groundwork of any depth by using great thicknesses of plaster usually causes problems. Where real contours in the ground are required, a core of expanded polystyrene lamina-tions should always be used. The plaster groundwork should then be run over this as nothing more than a light skim. Ceiling

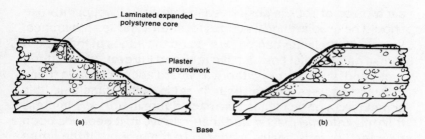

Contoured groundwork (a) straight cut contours, requiring a greater thickness of plaster than in (b) where the contours have been wire-brushed to the rough shape.

tiles are ideal for this work, as are some of the pieces used for packing.

To produce contoured groundwork, a full-size plan should be made of the diorama and the contours sketched onto this. Some guesswork has to be made as to where the contours of each lamination actually lie. The rule is – where the ground falls steeply they should be close together; where the slope is gentle they should be well apart. They can be cut out quite cleanly with a sharp craft knife and stuck to each other and the baseboard with white PVA glue. Once they are stuck in position they can either be plastered over directly, or they can be carved or wire-brushed to a closer approximation to the final section before plastering. The latter method has the advantage that the overall thickness of plaster is more uniform and generally thinner.

Plaster can be easily applied using a small trowel or a spatula, this being kept wet at all times by dipping it into water. To make sure it adheres, the base should be deeply scored in a criss-cross pattern with a heavy-duty craft knife. The main aim should be to get a good approximation to the shape of the ground required, without worrying too much about the actual finish. With a wet trowel the result should be fairly smooth anyway. If it isn't, it can be improved by dipping the end of a one-inch paintbrush into water and using this to smooth it out. The latter is actually very useful for creating small humps and hollows, and much easier to use than a trowel, which should be thought of mainly as a tool for transferring the bulk of plaster to the base.

At this stage, provision should be made for any items that have to be let into the plaster, such as rocks, trees, bushes, etc. Rocks should be pushed well down into the still wet plaster. As each piece of rock is positioned in this way, a wet paintbrush should be used around its edges to 'naturalise' its appearance. Some of the plaster can be pushed up the edges of the rock to form a natural fillet between the rock and the ground; in nature, rocks and earth mingle without any hard edges between them. Fences and trees can be similarly set in at the same time. It is sometimes a good idea to take each figure in turn and impress it lightly into the plaster and then remove it; it depends upon how the figure is finally anchored to the ground. If the figure has pegs under the feet, the usual practice is to drill corresponding holes in the groundwork when it is dry. Nonetheless, it is sometimes still quite useful to have the figure's position impressed in the groundwork. This can also be done with vehicles.

You will need to bear in mind the weight of vehicles. A heavy vehicle will not normally sit on the surface, except on concrete or tarmac, but will sink into it to an extent determined by its weight (and its distribution) and the softness of the ground. Even though this should be obvious, model vehicles are often seen sitting on the surface of soft ground!

At this point the groundwork can be left to set fully before the final surface texture is applied. As a starting point, it can be assumed that a grassy type of terrain is required.

In a small-scale diorama (1:72 or 1:76), a grassy effect can be obtained merely by brushing the terrain surface with PVA adhesive and sprinkling very find sand over it. When dry, the surplus can be shaken off and the surface painted in the appropriate colours, the effect of grass being suggested simply by texture and colour. The colours are best sprayed or air-brushed on to avoid sand being picked up in the hairs of a brush.

In larger scales, grass is often represented by means of 'flock' powder, obtainable from model railway shops. To lay this, the surface of the groundwork should be coated with thinned PVA adhesive and the powder sprinkled on. Gently blowing it removes the surplus and causes the remainder to stand up more naturally. The somewhat unnatural colour can be improved by overspraying it with more natural tints.

A much better, and more realistic method, is the use of 'scenery mat'. A West German product called Sander Struktur can be obtained in rolls from model railway shops. This has a brown paper backing and can be cut to size and fixed in place with PVA adhesive. The cut edges can be disguised by plastering over them, so causing the grass to merge into earth or rocky ground, for example. The colour is quite good but, again, it can be painted to any desired shade, either overall or in random patches, but this time a brush can safely be used. It is possible to create a bare patch or even a footpath merely by wetting the area in question, leaving it for a few minutes and then scraping away some flock with your fingernail.

Clumps of long, coarse grass are usually obtained by unpicking that rather hairy string known as 'sisal'. They can be dyed to a reasonable colour by using Boots cold water dyes, for example. It can then be glued in clumps into holes made in the groundwork. Other alternatives are bristles from old tooth-brushes, paint brushes or other domestic brushes and brooms.

Rocks were mentioned earlier and many dioramas can be given extra interest with at least a few of them, provided that some thought is given to their placing. It is possible to add just a few judiciously placed rocks of varying sizes or to have a massive outcrop as part of the scene.

One way of representing rocks it to use the real thing, though on a much smaller scale! It is quite possible to find some that are suitable for modelling in your own garden. Therefore, it pays to keep your eyes open at all times for such treasures and collect them as the opportunities occur. Another excellent material for model rocks, large or small, is 'cork bark', and a large packet can be obtained from a model railway shop for very little cost. It is possible to break off tiny pieces to sink into the plaster for small rocks or it is equally possible to build up veritable hills with the stuff! Its texture already suggests the nature of rugged, rocky terrain; it only needs colouring to improve its appearance. Nonetheless, it integrates well with plaster to give a variety of rocky effects.

Some materials for producing a variety of textural effects, from finely sieved sand, through stones of various sizes and kinds to cork boulders and slabs.

Mud in dioramas will generally be represented merely by colouring the basic plaster groundwork with, perhaps, a coat of varnish to suggest its wetness. Because mud is so 'plastic' it will be affected by everything that has passed over it. Rarely smooth, its surface will be churned up by the wheels of carts and trucks, by the hooves of horses, and by the feet of men. Any vehicle that finds itself in it is likely to have its wheels or tracks sunk well down. It is also likely to be liberally coated with the stuff. A way of relieving the tedium of mud is to include the odd, isolated, patch of green, remembering that what is now mud may have previously been a green field.

Sand is best represented by – sand! The type that comes from a builder's yard may well appear rather coarse at first sight, but it actually contains grains of every conceivable size, which can be easily separated out with a fine flour sieve. Another possible source of sand is the beach. In some parts of the country it is very fine and quite suitable for dioramas. A 'sandy' finish used by modeller John Hunter employs the soil residue that collects in the angle between the kerbstone and the road surface. This is very fine and can be sieved and sprinkled onto either wet plaster or plaster that has been given a coat of thinned PVA—a useful material at zero cost!

Snow can be represented with ordinary table salt, sprinkled over a white painted finish, the latter coated with PVA glue, or salts of Alum from the chemist, applied in a similar manner. Either way, the effect of the crystals is to give a sparkle to the snow, enhancing its realism. If a heavy covering of snow is required it can be applied by using thinned-down plaster. However, it may require a little trial and error to obtain a convincing effect. Freshly fallen snow, with some wind about,

Split dried lentils are easily placed onto a surface of PVA glue using the tip of a craft knife. Don't place them in lines but more randomly.

To represent the accretion produced by time, they should be 'grouted' with well thinned Polyfilla. They can then be painted as required. A dusting with the appropriate weathering powder can suggest moss.

creates some fantastic shapes. Where it meets a vertical surface, such as the wall of a house, it will rise up in a smooth curve.

A road surface may be just a rough, unpaved track, perhaps potholed, a cobbled street or a modern highway. The first of these may be just painted plaster with a few stones sunk in here and there, the second can be laid with split lentils and the third can be produced by painting a smooth surface (e.g. plastic card) the appropriate colour and adding markings with masks or stencils.

Indoor surfaces include floors, generally of stone, tiles or wood. It is possible to cut regular, or irregular, stones or tiles from thick plastic card and stick them down, either leaving a slight gap between them or grouting them after they have been painted with something like Polyfilla. Alternatively, they can be represented by spreading a very thin coat of Tetrion or a similar plaster onto the surface of the base and, when it has started to dry, using a pointed implement to mark out the required pattern. When this is properly dry the tiles or stones can be painted.

The same principle can be applied to flagstones used in outdoor scenes. However, the divisions between adjacent stones will usually acquire dirt and moss. This can be represented by brushing on a wash of well-thinned, dirty green enamel or oil paint and then immediately wiping it off. This will have the effect of weathering the stones themselves and leaving the appearance of moss between them. Alternatively, it is possible, with care, to brush an appropriate colour from the

One can be a bit fancy and lay alternate planks in different veneers. After sanding to a smooth finish, a coat of button polish (shellac), followed by a couple of coats of satin varnish, sanding between coats, will give a pleasing result.

range of Carr's weathering powders into the gaps between the stones.

Simple planked wooden floors are quite easy to lay using marquetry veneers. These are available from good model shops or craft shops, in a very large variety of different woods. Whereas, in modern houses floorboards are laid in a regular pattern rather like bricks, in earlier times this was not always so. The pattern may well appear quite random. The planks should be cut in strips of scale width and of slightly differing lengths, using a steel rule and a sharp knife. They can be stuck down with PVA glue, the excess being wiped off immediately with a damp cloth, otherwise any varnishes applied later will be patchy. A very nice finish can be obtained by using a couple of coats of shellac (button polish), rubbing down between each coat, with satin varnish applied last of all.

While more ambitious buildings will have to be scratchbuilt, some simple structures, as well as resin-cast ruins, are available in kit form.

To work on a building, ruined or otherwise, means a 'straight' paint job first of all. This produces a 'clean' model in the appropriate colours.

Buildings and other structures

Buildings can be bought in kit form or made from scratch, using plastic card and balsa wood as the main materials. It is rare to model a whole building because of the matter of size. Many dioramas manage with just a corner or facade as a suitable 'prop' for the figures and vehicles that are the main components of the scene. Because of this, several makers produce either portions of ruined buildings or complete but much smaller structures. Such makers include Francois Verlinden with his resin-cast kits and Italeri with their range of plastic kits. Both have a range of supporting accessories.

However, top modellers usually make their own ruins, with a core of expanded polystyrene covered with a thin skim of plaster, into which suitable detail is cut with the tip of an appropriate instrument, such as a screwdriver blade. Openings have to be cut for doors and windows, the remains of which are usually fabricated from balsawood strips with clear plastic sheet for broken window panes. There will be a substantial debris around the site, unless there has been a thorough cleaning-up operation since the bombardment that put the building into its present state.

A demolished brick wall can be represented with fragments of the real thing, by pounding an actual brick into oblivion with a heavy hammer and strewing the fragments around the diorama. These should be supplemented by shattered timbers from the floors and roof, again from balsa wood. Useful items such as lamp posts and signs are available in kit form and can be used, easier than making them from scratch. John Hunter is a master at this type of diorama and takes great pains to get the

A dirty paint colour can be run into cracks with a fine brush and weathering powders can be added here and there, for example to represent the blackening caused by fire or to suggest a growth of moss.

right amount of destruction into his creations, whichever side they are viewed from!

Weathering is important if a building is to look authentic. A freshly painted building must be 'dirtied up' somewhat, a task that can be carried out using some of Carr's extensive range of 'weathering powders'. Some of these are useful for applying coats of moss, streaks of rust, muddiness or a sooty appearance to various parts of the building. Dry-brushing can also be applied to edges here and there – that is flicking an almost dry brush against these edges with a colour slightly lighter than the basic colour. For some surfaces, a dirty wash or oil-paint can be run into engraved detail and the surface wiped clean(ish!) to represent the accumulation of natural dirt.

Trees, brushes and other vegetation
Many dioramas include some form of vegetation. Starting with trees and working down the scale, only small trees should be

A detail of another of John Hunter's dioramas that shows the effective use of 'Woodland Scenics' foliage (from model railway shops) used in conjunction with dry twigs from the garden.

attempted because of the problems of scale size. There are several ways in which these can be made, the use of a twisted wire 'armature' being a favourite.

This method uses a bundle of wires, some thick and some thin, twisted up tightly to represent the trunk and being progressively unwound at the top to form the branches, and often to some extent at the bottom too for a few roots. When the desired formation is obtained, some soft solder can be run in here and there for strength and the whole thing plastered over using either epoxy putty (Milliput), Tetrion plaster or Plastic Padding. Before this is set the bark can be engraved with the tip of a sharp tool. The 'bare' tree is then painted. Leaves can be obtained in packets from model railway shops, and there is a range by Carr's which are actually minute pieces of coloured foam plastic. If the branches are coated with thinned PVA glue, the leaves can be sprinkled on and the surplus shaken off for a quite realistic effect.

Another method uses a piece of natural twig (another trip into the garden!); this forms the trunk and main branches. The foliage can be formed from plastic lichen or from 'teased out' wire-wool to which plastic leaves have been attached after spraying it with photo-mount adhesive. Bushes can be made in the latter way, or from plastic lichen.

The 'wire armature' method of making trees (a) a thick bundle of twisted copper wire forms the trunk, being progressively unravelled to form the branches and roots. (b) The armature is covered in a thick layer of Milliput or tetrion which is engraved (c) to form the bark pattern.

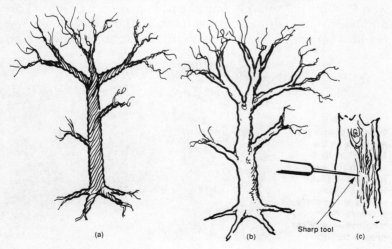

Sharp tool

(a) (b) (c)

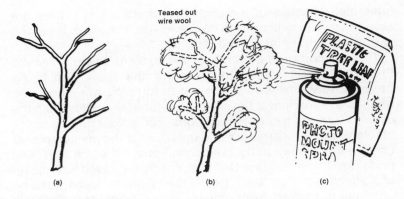

Teased out
wire wool

(a)   (b)   (c)

An alternative method of making a tree (a) find a suitable dry twig in the
garden and trim it to the required shape (b) tease out some of the wire-
wool to a fluffy shape and attach with PVA glue. (c) Spray with photo
mount adhesive and sprinkle plastic leaves on.

There are some excellent etched metal kits for plants;
especially good are the aquatic and jungle plants produced by
Verlinden Productions, though Scale Link also have a good
range. These are just snipped out of the fret with scissors, bent
to shape with fingers and tweezers, and painted and epoxied
into holes drilled in the groundwork.

Other forms of vegetation, excluding grass which has
already been discussed, are creepers on buildings (such as ivy)
and growths such as moss, found in damp situations. Any easy
way of representing growths of this sort is as follows. On the
wall of the building, the form of the growth is painted on thinly
with PVA glue. Then very fine plastic leaves (e.g. Carr's willow
and beech) are sprinkled on and the surplus shaken off. The
result is very effective. The colour of moss can be represented

Smaller plants are
available in the
form of etched
metal frets, each
part of the plant
being detached
with a sharp knife or
scissors. Assembly
with cyanoacrylate
glue is possible.

A heavy growth, such as ivy, is very easy to achieve in just two steps. In the first of these the pattern of the creeper is applied in PVA glue. When dry this glue becomes clear, so will not be visible.

by the use of green weathering powders or very thick mossy growths can be made using the method just described for creepers.

Water

Representing water offers a fascinating challenge to the modeller. There are four basic ways of doing it.

The first method is by far the easiest and is very effective if done properly. The deception is carried out by painting the area of the stream bed (assuming that this is what is being modelled) with patches and streaks of browns and greens of different shades – dark where the water is to be deep, light where it is to be shallow. Either enamels or acrylics can be used for this. When it is dry a number of coats of gloss varnish are then applied until the desired appearance is obtained. Half a dozen coats is usually enough, though Jack Higgs, in his midget submarine diorama, used no less than 22 coats over an underpainting of Humbrol enamels!

In the second step, fine plastic leaves, such as Carr's 'Willow and Beech' are sprinkled over the wall so that some adhere to the PVA pattern; the surplus is simply shaken off.

This midget submarine diorama by a leading exponent of World War Two dioramas, Jack Higgs, has a most realistic sea effect that was created by laying no less than 22 coats of varnish over an underpainting of Humbrol enamels.

The second method is rather more elaborate but is very good if underwater objects, including human feet, are to be included. It is based on the pouring of successive thin layers of casting resin. The area of water must be designed to contain this liquid and the bed is painted in the desired colours first; any rocks or plants, etc, on the bottom must also be in position before the first pouring. Using paint or dyes, a greater impression of depth can be obtained if the first layer is dyed the most, the second less and subsequent layers even less or not at all. The resin should be covered to exclude dust while it is drying.

The third method involves pouring PVA glue over the painted stream bed and leaving it to dry out. It tends to dry clear, but becomes more opaque as the thickness builds up. It is quite good for representing 'troubled water', especially if strings of tube cement are laid over the top and touches of white paint applied.

The final method is applicable where water in extreme motion is required. Plaster is used, being applied with a trowel but whipped up into the required shape with a one-inch paint brush, the end of which is dipped occasionally into water. It is

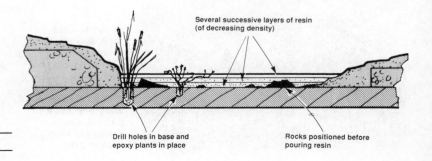

Several successive layers of resin (of decreasing density)

Drill holes in base and epoxy plants in place

Rocks positioned before pouring resin

possible to get excellent waves with a little practice. When it is dry and has been primed with matt white enamel, the final effect is obtained by painting and varnishing. Colours varying from mid-blue to deep blue-green should be applied quite wetly so that the darker hue accumulates in the troughs. White paint is then flicked onto the peaks of the waves to represent the 'white horses'. The effect is completed with a coat or two of satin varnish.

A flat calm stretch of water produced by Barry Bowen, using successive coats of PVA glue over a painted base. The bridge is also noteworthy, being constructed from Tetrion plaster on an expanded polystyrene core. The stonework detail can easily be engraved using nothing more sophisticated than the tip of a screwdriver blade! Also look at that superb tree in the background—twisted wire and Tetrion with minute leaves added!

7   PAINTING TO PLEASE

TED TAYLOR

A more appropriate title for this chapter could be 'painting to impress'; so many times I have had to judge models that have had many extra features, such as completely fabricated cockpit interiors, beautiful conversions to another type and, sometimes, a scratchbuilt item, that for sheer amount of work alone, should win a prize. However, all have lacked one special feature – a good paint job – and so have been eliminated.

To achieve a reasonable finish that will be pleasing and catch the eye of the onlooker, there are certain basic rules that must be followed by newcomer or expert alike:

1. Cleanliness.
2. Finish of the surface to be painted.
3. Patience to wait for the paint to dry.
4. Perseverance to overcome any problems.

These are not 'golden rules', just methods I have found work for me.

Cleanliness

This means *everything*, although if using a brush you can by-pass some things, but the use of an airbrush means all criteria have to be fulfilled.

A clean work surface is essential. I find a roll of kitchen towel very useful; a couple of strips laid across a clean work top tends to collect any over-spray and soak it up rather than letting it bounce back. It is also cheap enough to discard after each painting session.

Tools must also be clean and this should be done immediately after a paint session rather than before the next, as paint has a nasty habit of drying out, which then becomes very hard to remove! For brushes I have two small fish paste jars which are held in position on my workbench with Plasticine, both half filled with Polyclens-Plus, a brush cleaner not a 'thinner'. As soon as the job is done, dip the brush in the nearest jar, then known as the dirty pot, to remove the excess paint. When clear, gently wipe with kitchen towel, dip back into the second pot for a final rinse, before gently drying with a paper towel. Pop it back into your storage box and it should last for years—that's if it's a good brush (if it's a cheap one don't expect it to last too long)!

For airbrushes you can buy aerosol cans of cleaning fluid from your model shop, but I have a simple method that always leaves the tool ready to use. After spraying a colour, the jar is removed and a second jar with Polyclens is attached. A little is then sprayed through the brush to remove the paint. When it comes through clear, hang up the airbrush with the jar still attached until the next time, when you can simply blow the remains of the cleaner through, before attaching your paint jar. If you have a side cup fitting on your airbrush, a couple of brushfuls of cleaner can be blown through to good effect.

Before spraying, wash your model in a bowl of warm water with just a little washing up liquid added. Next use an old shaving brush to help remove any release oil or sanding dust from the surface. Rinse under a cold tap to flush out all the soap, shake out as much water as possible and leave to dry overnight, without wiping, as this can put more dust back and create 'static' which will attract dust.

There may be dust particles in a paint finish that have come from your clothing, so avoid wearing wool, nylon is preferable. My rule is that if you can see fluff on your clothes then you will see them on the model. The same applies to carpets, so try to use a room without any, or spread brown paper around the work area.

Surface finish

In most cases the plastic parts of your kit have a perfect surface to paint on, i.e. even, smooth, and hard. Unfortunately, we often have to spoil that surface during construction, so how do we get it back? By sanding or filing the affected areas.

Remember you cannot sand plastic that has been softened by glue, so let it harden for 24 hours at least, then give a light rub over with a fine grade of paper to see if you need any filler, or to eliminate any unevenness. When you are satisfied, take some wet and dry paper, I use '1000 Grade', and gently polish the surface with a circular motion back to a silky finish. I rarely use my eyes to check a surface, as the tips of my fingers can tell me if it is sufficiently silky.

Grades of paper Although we all call it sandpaper, it is best to ask for Garnet Paper which can be recognised by its reddish brown colour. Try to buy three grades; No. 2 for sanding heavy construction work, No. 6 to level surface joints and No. 9 to finish off with. Lubrasil or freecut are also excellent papers for plastic working, for which there are two grades, 320 and 240. The finest grade will give a surface good enough to brush paint onto.

Wet and dry paper, if used dry, will lift only the smallest amount, as it clogs easily, but when used wet remains clear and is very effective. Try to get three grades if you can: 600 grit is good for heavy work and is the roughest you will need; 1000 grit is good for any plastic and will give a surface good enough to spray onto; 1200 grit is good for rubbing down gloss paint that may have run or got fluff in it; I also use it to give that final polish to the plastic when I want a super gloss or silver finish.

If you can't get the finest grade, then tear a small corner off the sheet and rub it over a part of the sheet you want to use. This will effectively reduce the grit to half its size, i.e. 600 grit will be reduced to 1200 grit, and you can feel the difference!

Types of paint

Most model shops stock Humbrol enamel paints which are of very good quality, easy to use, and quick drying. If you brush paint then I can recommend these. Those in the *Basic* range have a fairly coarse pigment and some are not truly authentic while matt finishes are dead matt. The *Authentic* range of paints are usually a little more expensive, but the pigment is much finer and therefore easier to spray to a very fine edge. These are available in US Navy and Air Force colours, along with RAF and

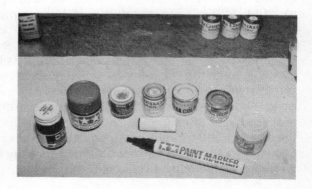

Various brands of modelling paints.

other Air Forces. Most have that nice egg shell finish which I think looks so good on a scale model. All Humbrol paints should be thinned with white spirit or Humbrol's own thinners, to BS 245 standard.

There are specialist paints available such as Xtracolor. These are made to exact matches in use for most Air Forces of the world; such as the Federal Standards 595A range, and British Standard ranges and German RAL range. These have a gloss finish so decals can be put straight on, and matt or semi-matt varnishes used to hide decal film. This is an excellent method but you do, of course, have to be more skilled in the use of gloss paint. Spraying is the primary aim of this range but they can be brushed quite effectively. White spirit, again, is the correct thinner to use.

Acrylic paints The finish of acrylic paints is always silky smooth and they dry very quickly, but some of the solvents used are quite pungent. Most are advertised as water soluble which means that can be washed off with water. They are not, however, thinned with water, you must use the manufacturers' own brand of thinners. Tamiya paints are available in some larger shops and the Gunze Sangyo range is now being distributed in the UK. Both these ranges though, are not as big as the enamel ones.

Cellulose paints These are mostly used by car and truck modellers, but beware if you are a newcomer. Cellulose will burn or melt the plastic and will also ruin any enamel paint underneath it. If you must use cellulose, make sure the ventilation is adequate as the fumes are highly inflammable. When you spray you must only mist the first couple of coats on and gradually build up the paint finish so the solvent evaporates rather than dissolving the plastic.

Its advantages are a super quick drying time, it can be T'cut and polished, and the shine can, with practice, be eye-catching.

The disadvantages are that it can only be sprayed, never brushed, as it is harmful to plastic and enamel paint. You can, of course, brush or spray enamel paint over cellulose without damage.

Silver finishes Always the most difficult to achieve if we really want 'metal', i.e. bare aluminium etc.

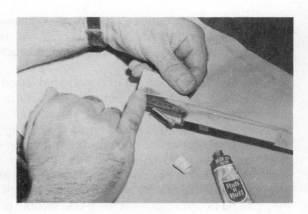

Rub 'n Buff being applied with a finger. When finished it will be masked and any excess removed with a cloth moistened with thinners.

Several silver paints are available for silver dope or paint simulation and each modeller has his own choice of brand. I like Humbrol's No. 11 silver for oleos etc. Aluminium is made in several ranges and each job may require a different one.

There are, at present, two methods that I use, the first is Rub n' Buff.

This is a 'paste' in a tube which can be applied with a piece of sponge or, as I prefer, with your finger. Spread it out thinly and keep buffing with your finger until the surface takes on the required shine. I add a little more realism to this with a fine smear of Zebrite grate polish as a final coat, which imparts a deep metallic finish. The finish is quite permanent providing you don't handle it, but any paint brushed over it will mix and spoil it. To overcome this I now use Johnson's Klear which is acrylic, and a coat of this seals it and prevents wear.

The second is with Sn.J spray metal. This should be sprayed on in about three fine misted coats leaving 5–10 minutes between each. The paint must be left for at least one hour, then

Both types of silver finish and the Zebrite Grate Polish.

some of the panels may be buffed up with the polishing powder supplied, to any degree of shine you wish (I have made some bits look like chrome). But the powder buffing should be done before 12 hours have elapsed as the paint then becomes very hard. In fact, you can brush or spray other paints over it without them mixing.

The basic silver can be tinted with a few drops of enamel paint mixed in i.e. titanium, to simulate other metals – some other colours are available.

Decals can be applied straight onto this finish and finger prints, if any, can be rubbed off. The finish is tough, and masking and sellotape can be used on it without damaging the surface. This has got to be the best silver/metal finish I have ever found.

Both these methods have their uses, but one thing they have in common is that the base surface of the plastic must be perfect. The plastic as it comes out of the mould is good enough, but any work on it will need careful cleaning up and a final polish with 1200 grade wet and dry paper to restore the surface.

To get the best out of silver paint from a tin, dip the brush in, then wipe it on the lip a couple of times, wait a second or two, then load the brush from the lip and spread on the model. Try not to brush more than once if you want a real shine; each further brush gives a more matt result, which enables you to get the finish you want.

Brush painting

The majority of model painting is still done by hand with a brush bought along with the model. Most of the brushes available are round bristle and, while a reasonable finish can be

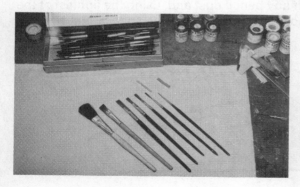

A range of brushes that will do most jobs; the largest is my dust remover, the next is a small flattie for applying varnish or 'Klear'.

attained, it won't be the best possible. As an example, if you were painting your front door, would you use a round brush? Of course not, you would use a 3in. flat brush. On a smaller scale this still applies, however, brush widths are graduated from ⅛ in. to ¼ in.

Sable hair is the best, with a bristle length of approximately ¾in. In careful hands this type of brush will follow a camouflage line without rolling or springing to give a really sharp edge and, with practice, can give a level finish almost equal to an airbrush.

Most tins of paint come with a consistency to suit brush work, but various colours, such as greens and browns, will benefit from a little extra thinner being added. I try to achieve a consistency that will even out on the surface with only one stroke of the brush; add one or two drops of thinner until you are happy, and test it out on the inside of a wing. Never overload your brush as it will start to dry and 'pull' before you can spread it all. Where complicated surfaces are concerned, always brush the difficult corners first, then tidy up with an overall finish using a half loaded brush, which is spread as quickly as possible, using brush strokes in one direction only. Avoid over brushing any well spread paint as, at this stage, it will start to dry in seconds, forming a skin. A second brush stroke will form lumps, or even brush marks.

With each stroke try to cover the width of a wing or up to a particular panel line. With the next brushful, start ⅛ in. away then brush it back to the last piece to avoid a ridge at the join. This is particularly important with gloss paints.

When tackling a camouflage scheme, such as the USAF S.E. Asia pattern, draw all the outlines with a soft pencil over the whole aircraft and mark each area with an initial to denote its colour. Brush off any pencil dust and, using the lightest of the upper surface colours, start to fill in the spaces. Put the first

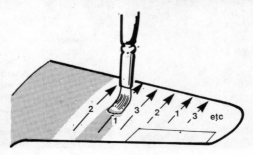

Note how paint is spread outwards from stroke number one.

stroke just away from your line, then brush it out to the line as quickly as possible before filling in the middle. When the first colour is on, leave overnight to dry. Next day, pencil in any line you may have missed and repeat the process with the next lightest colour, taking care to cover the pencil line along the edge of the first colour. Again leave overnight to dry before finishing with the darkest colour.

I take each colour below the level of the underside colour, right along the fuselage to avoid any unsightly gaps later. The underside dividing line is usually wavy and here you could run into difficulties if you try to be too accurate, because of the paint beginning to dry. Therefore, aim for a quickly applied line which is fairly accurate, then fill in with a wide brush.

Masking

Masking is one of the most important parts of spray painting but it is not an exact science. You can use several methods to do various jobs. There are a few rules to bear in mind: 1) Any masking tape in use should be kept in a plastic bag; *never* put it down on a work bench as dust and dirt will stick to the edges. 2) Ideally you should wait 24 hours before masking newly applied paint. 3) Ensure the tape is Low Tac or it will pull the paint off. If you want to 'de tac' your tape, rub each strip up and down over the edge of a table or desk lightly. 4) Always mask the smallest or easiest area, so paint nose cones, fin tips, wheel bays etc. first. 5) When applying masking tape, always position with a very light touch and when correctly aligned, you can firm the edges using a cocktail stick to push

Mask off nose cones using narrow tape which will conform to the contours easily. To get the divide, cover the remainder with wider tape.

Run tape over table edge to remove some of the tackiness.

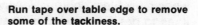

The ½in. tape along the fuselage is used to get the sharp line accurate and the fin covered with a piece of kitchen towel cut to size and edged with wide tape. This is folded over the fin and fixed to ½in. tape to avoid damage to prepainted fin.

Two ways to mask the cockpit: Tissue paper is carefully tucked into the cockpit before seats are added. The nearest aircraft has the canopy in place and carefully masked with Scotch 810 Magic Tape which was cut in situ and the edges firmly pressed down. Note how canopy area is sprayed black before main colour is added—this saves the tedious job of painting the frame interiors by hand.

the tape into nooks and crannies plus panel lines. 6) Always cut tape on a piece of glass with a sharp knife and a steel rule, for a clean sharp edge. 7) Never use Sellotape on a painted surface; it is much too sticky and will lift the paint. However, I do use it for canopies where you need to see the edge to be cut around the 'glass' part.

Spray painting
Much has been written on using airbrushes, but I have found that I have learned more from practice, referring back to a book when a problem occurs. However, here are some general guide lines to get you started in the right direction.

Firstly, choose a good airbrush to suit your particular job. If you just want an overall colour on a tank, then you can buy one of the proprietary spray guns which are fairly cheap. The Badger 250 is one such gun and Humbrol and Revell also produce an equivalent. These are however only spray guns and have a very limited usage.

To achieve the finishes that we all see and admire on the competition tables you will need an 'airbrush'. This is a far more finely engineered tool and, as such, can be used to get more precise control over paint flow and air mixture. To give you that very fine edge required for a camouflage scheme, both types, gun or brush, will give a nice even finish which you can be proud of, so the choice is yours.

When you come to buy an air brush, you will find the choice quite staggering. The top of the range models are generally meant for studio use on art work, or retouching photos with inks or watercolour paints. These airbrushes are much too fine for enamel paints as they will clog up quite easily and most have side cups which tend to spill when you move around the model.

The two most common airbrush manufacturers found in model shops are De Vilbliss and Badger. De Vilbliss make the Sprite and Sprite Major, both of which have one single control button which you press down to release the air and pull back to release the paint. This is called a double action airbrush and, while it can have some advantages, I find that I am unable to keep my finger in one position for very long and the paint line tends to vary in width.

Badger produce an airbrush of this type—the '150' or '100', but they also make a '200' which has a paint jar below the gun and a screw operated needle which regulates the paint flow and therefore, the line width, so once you have set the thickness you require, it will remain constant, leaving your finger free to control the air flow. Personally, I think that the Badger 200 is the best airbrush for plastic model making, as it will spray a line fine enough to do a 1:72 scale camouflage line, and wide enough to cover a 1:32 scale aircraft in fairly quick time. Always buy three or four spare jars, you will need them!

A small piece of 10thou. card can be cut to shape along any of the four edges, in this case an F-4 Phantom Wing for the British Grey scheme. The card is held in position to get a straight line on a short strip.

The wheel bays have been painted and are being masked by the main undercarriage doors, held in place with Blu Tack. The nose bay will be filled with Blu Tack as the door hinges preclude fitting.

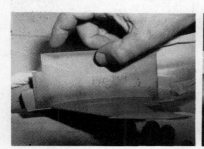

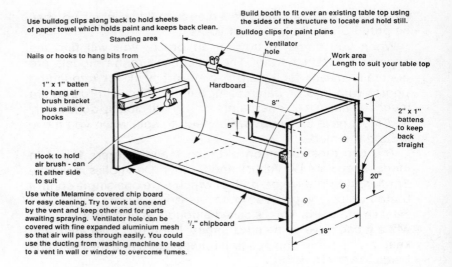

Use bulldog clips along back to hold sheets of paper towel which holds paint and keeps back clean.

Build booth to fit over an existing table top using the sides of the structure to locate and hold still.

Standing area

Bulldog clips for paint plans

Nails or hooks to hang bits from

Ventilator hole

Work area
Length to suit your table top

1" x 1" batten to hang air brush bracket plus nails or hooks

Hardboard

8"

2" x 1" battens to keep back straight

5"

Hook to hold air brush - can fit either side to suit

20"

Use white Melamine covered chip board for easy cleaning. Try to work at one end by the vent and keep other end for parts awaiting spraying. Ventilator hole can be covered with fine expanded aluminium mesh so that air will pass through easily. You could use the ducting from washing machine to lead to a vent in wall or window to overcome fumes.

$\frac{1}{2}$" chipboard

18"

'Let us spray'

Firstly, make sure you can hold all the parts to be sprayed. With an aircraft it can be the masked areas, like the nose cone, or you can stick a finger in the exhaust pipe. With fuel tanks, bombs and wheels, for instance, drill a small hole in an 'unseen' surface and push a cocktail stick in to make an effective handle. Stand them in a block of Plasticine after painting. Wooden clothes pegs can be adapted to make good clamps to hold parts by lugs and pins. Cut the ends with a razor saw to give a sharp angle to get close up with.

For car or truck bodies and cabs, wire coat hangers are ideal. Cut off two bottom corners to make U shapes, and bend an inch

Cocktail sticks being inserted into fuel tank pylons. When painted they will stand in the plasticine block which has been covered with cling film.

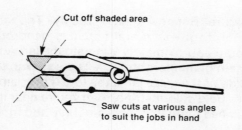

Cut off shaded area

Saw cuts at various angles to suit the jobs in hand

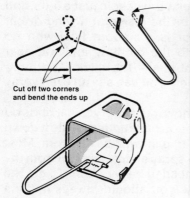

Cut off two corners and bend the ends up

Note pencilled outline to each colour section, spray as close to these as possible. Don't worry if you overstep the mark as the next colour can re-establish the correct line.

over at the ends to 90°. ³/₄in. tape can be used to fix the ends to the interior of the body.

I quite often use a strip of 1in. × ¹/₈in. wood lathe covered with double-sided tape to hold tiny parts etc. Only uncover as much tape as you need and it will last a long time.

Draw out your camouflage pattern with a soft pencil and initial each colour section. Then, when you are sure everything is ready, mounted and clean, you can mix up your paint.

Mixing quantities

How much thinners? is probably the most asked question, with no single answer; there are many criteria such as colour, temperature and purpose. Let's deal with temperature first as this is easily controlled. Paints in general are designed to spray at 65–75°F. This gives time for the paint to even out before drying; anything below 65° takes longer to dry and so could run (if it is gloss). Anything above 75° tends to dry much quicker with not enough time to even out. If you are using matt colours it is not much of a problem, but for a good gloss finish it is critical.

All good airbrushing books say the paint should have a

'creamy mixture'. But how thick is creamy? The way I achieve a good spray mix to give an overall colour is to thoroughly stir the tinlet, and pour approximately ⅛ in. into the jar. Add about half as much again of thinners and mix. Dip a stick in the paint and place it inside of the glass jar at the top. If the paint runs down easily, with a bold colour stripe, then you're near it but if it runs slowly, you need more thinners—but only add three drops at a time.

Put your jar on the airbrush, open the needle just a little, and test the spray on an old model or the inside of a wing or car body. What you are looking for is a smooth flow with no splatters. You can also listen to the air flow and will hear splatters beginning if your paint is still too thick. Add more thinners, three drops at a time, until you can see an even spray and hear a smooth hiss of air.

When you have got it right, see how much is in your jar and you can work out how much thinners you have added. Write it down for future reference as every tin of paint will be different. Most colours differ also: blues tend to spray almost straight from the tin, while reds and yellows will need to be very thin. To get the best effect from red and yellow you should always apply a white undercoat. Use this standard mix to spray the first colour, carefully but not too precisely, then leave to dry. To get a feathered edge, you need a slightly thinner paint mix; pour a tiny amount of paint into a jar and again thin by stages, until the paint will flow with the needle almost closed. If you now hold the airbrush a half inch from the surface you should get a very fine line. Use the brush like a pencil, travelling back and forth along your pencil lines until the colour builds up solid. Then continue to widen the line to approximately ⅛ in. around the

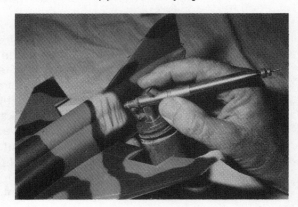

Approaching the final stage, a standard mix is used to fill in the second colour. Note how close the airbrush is to the surface and the narrow outline sprayed around the edges first. The fine lines are where I have tested the mix before starting.

A fine strip of tape is cut from 1in. strip and laid on the base light colour. After adding main colour it can be removed to reveal a base colour outline to the walkway.

edges, pointing the gun towards the centre all the time to avoid overspray on the first colour. Now add a drop more paint to make a standard mix and fill in the bulk of the area. Repeat for further colours but leave each colour mix in the jar, just to retouch the odd spot missed, until you are satisfied with your work. If you have only mixed a small amount, you can throw the paint away, rather than pouring it back in the tin. Wash all jars with Poly Clens.

Hints and tips

Any feathered edge colours sprayed freehand can be sprayed as soon as the first colour can be handled. You don't have to wait overnight as with masked or brushed colours.

Be economical with your brush; keep the needle closed to suit your needs and your paint will dry as you put it on—I call it dry spraying. Don't be tempted to open the needle more than needed for the sake of speed or impatience, because paint will flow too fast and make the surface wet. This takes longer to dry (like hours) and you will probably have sprayed half of your room as well!

If the paint is taking a long time to dry, take the airbrush, minus paint jar, and 'spray' air over the surface. You can watch the paint dry...yes I know it is boring!

If I need just a small amount of paint and I have a half empty tin, I mix thinners in the tin to the required consistency. You can then use the airbrush without the jar, by pressing the air button and holding the paint tube in the tin. This will suck up a small amount, which can be sprayed in the normal manner. It is surprising how far a tubeful will go!

One important tip is to have good lights to work under – you are sure to miss bits if you can't see properly. Remember that under normal household lights, the colours of the paint will vary from those on the real aircraft or car in normal daylight. So try to work near a window or, if you have strip lighting, use 'colour matching' type tubes which are as close to daylight as you can get.

Gloss painting

With the introduction of Xtracolor, which is a gloss paint, it is even more important for aircraft modellers to acquire the knack of using it; it used to be mostly truck and car modellers who had to learn how to spray a good gloss finish!

In general all the parts must be extra clean, for which a goat mop is handy, and make sure you have a good light source. Good gloss paint should usually be a bit thinner than most matt finishes and you should aim to cover a larger area in one pass. Therefore, your brush will need to be opened a little more and you will have to spray from 5–8 in. away for a truck cab, or car body. If the base plastic is white, or a colour close to the colour required, then an undercoat is not needed (white is a good base for reds and yellows anyway). If you are going to make a complete change, then try applying a base coat which is close to the colour required. Then you can probably get away with one quite thin top coat. If you want to go from black, or very dark, to white, you can use Revell's aerosol cans of basic colour. This is a cellulose-based undercoat but is super fast drying and is safe to use on plastic. Make several passes, building up to a strong white colour which will be silky smooth when dry. This should be the finish to aim for with any undercoat. Do not use matt paint if you can help it as the

Coats of paint magnified

Semi-gloss undercoat

1st coat of gloss levels the surface

Matt undercoat

Note the advantages of using a semi-gloss undercoat.

1st coat of gloss will not fill the spaces

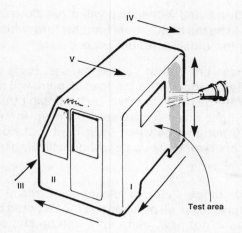

Test area

pigment size is quite large; it takes a lot of gloss paint to fill the gaps between to get a level surface that will reflect light evenly.

As with matt paint, use the underside of a mudguard etc to achieve the correct consistency by adding small amounts of thinners. Then choose the back of the cab, or narrow part of a car body to start on. Make even passes along one side, across the front and back, along the other side to the start. I like to make the passes up and down keeping them short, but always hold your model under a light so you can see the reflections as the paint levels out. Do the roof last of all, taking care not to over spray the sides. If you have separate doors or bonnet (hood), then spray them separately as it's easier to make one or two quick passes to cover an area that size. For instance, I always spray Italeri truck cabs as individual pieces, then assemble carefully later. However, if construction is difficult, do that first before cleaning up for painting.

Problems that can arise

'Orange peel' finish This can happen for two reasons. Firstly, the paint may be just a little too thick. Therefore add just a few drops of thinners and test spray a little patch. Watch for a few seconds to see it levels out; if it doesn't, add more. You can also open the needle a bit more if you think the consistency is right. The secret is to watch for the paint globules to break and even out. Once it seems smooth, move onwards. If you notice a bad patch and it's fresh, hold the gun away a little and give a light, very short burst, and with luck it will break down. The second reason could be too high a room temperature, which means the paint skins too quickly. Adjust accordingly

Paint runs These are due to several causes. Paint too thin, too much applied, temperature too low, so paint will not dry quick enough. If the paint is very thin and you can't thicken it, then make very light quick passes and build up in several coats, allowing 10 minutes between each coat, but no more. Also, apply no more than three coats without allowing the full drying time.

Bits in the paint surface Refer to 'cleanliness', mentioned earlier, and if you have taken all precautions then it could be your paint tin. If the tin is not new, there may well be bits of dried paint lurking below the surface. In this case, thin the paint to spray consistency and strain through a very fine wire mesh, but don't use a nylon stocking or you will get fluff in the paint instead. The best answer however is to buy a new tin.

General problems

Runs in gloss paint, too much applied at one pass or too thin. Solution: move airbrush faster or further away, close needle a little, add a little more paint.

Unable to get a fine line (feathered edge), paint splattering. Solution: thin paint until it will flow with needle almost closed and hold airbrush approx ½in. from surface. Your brush will sometimes dry up in this situation, but don't panic, stand back, open the needle and blast a drop of paint through gradually. Close needle back to position required and start again. This is one of the problems we all get!

Thinned paint blows away, paint is too thin and airbrush is too near. Solution: move brush back or add a little more paint to the mix.

A little paint has crept under the masking tape. Solution: a cotton bud or tip of cocktail stick moistened with Ronson lighter fluid will remove it before it hardens (which is why you take the tape off early). If it has hardened, mask new colour with card then touch up old colour with a short burst on the brush.

Unwanted paint on canopy. Solution: wait until the paint is just dry, but not hard. A clean pointed wooden cocktail stick can then remove it, without damage, if used carefully.

I find it best to remove masking tape as soon as you can safely handle the model but take care or you will lift earlier paint and even 'string' the edge of the paint just applied. Note how the tape is folded right back on its self—this reduces the danger of lifting, and how it is pulled back at a slight angle—this reduces the damage to an edge.

This aircaft has had the underside sprayed first then masked with narrow short lengths of tape. Note how carefully it is being removed.

Aerosol cans

For those of us who don't own an airbrush, painting can be a problem. However, there are plenty of aerosol cans on the market, some large and others small enough to handle one model. These 'Mini-sprays' are very useful.

Always shake the can very well until the ball agitator inside is really clattering around. Then let is stand for half a minute for the bubbles to burst. As the nozzles are wide, fairly large amounts of paint will come out, so hold the can approximately 1 ft. away and make a fast, but even, pass along the whole of a car body side. Do this once more if necessary. You can then go a little slower on the other side. If you have put a little too much on, you can keep turning the body on your home-made handle to stop gravity causing a run, until a skin forms. I have got some excellent results from these cans and I have seen some finishes that look good enough for that airbrushed look!

Summary

Make sure you have done your ground work carefully. Get the paint consistency correct and, using great care, spray fast light coats. Keep an eye on the surfaces for problems that might develop and stop if it's going wrong. Be patient and you will soon achieve a standard you once could only dream of! Good painting!

8　DETAILING AND WEATHERING

KEN JONES

Many modellers are completely satisfied with constructing a model kit straight from the box, happy with what the manufacturer supplies, and literally adding nothing but the paint to finish the job. However, there are also many who just cannot simply build a model straight from the box and add a host of extra details, or 'chop' the model about into something different.

The same is true of weathering, which is not to everyone's taste, some modellers preferring a 'showroom' finish for their efforts, making the true goal of modelling – realism – take a back seat. Never lose sight of the fact that we are endeavouring to create, in miniature, a facsimile of the real thing, whether we build it from a kit or from scratch. In this short chapter, I will attempt to offer my views on two often controversial subjects – detailing and weathering.

Why add details?
The simple answer to this question is, 'to make it different to everyone else's!' Take, for example, a model aeroplane built by yourself and an identical model built by your friend. Both are the same scale – 1 : 72 – and, to be bang up to date, ESCI's MiG-29 Fulcrum, the Soviet fighter that impressed the crowds with its aerobatic performance at the 1988 Farnborough airshow. After collecting photographs published in the specialist aviation press, you add ILS aerials to the nose of your model and also fit the Swiftrod antenna to the right rear tailplane. Your friend does not. Whose aircraft do you think would be the more authentic because of the added detail? Yet still modellers do not attempt to include even the basic detail necessities to their efforts.

The addition of extra details is fun and rewarding. There are specialist manufacturers producing such extras for all forms of modelling, and these come in etched metal, cast white metal, injection moulded plastic, polyurethane and polyester resins,

The starboard tailfin of a MiG 29UB shows the Swift Rod antenna and static discharge wick on the rudder—details such as these can be added easily in 1:72 scale, especially if using etched brass PP Aeroparts.

etc., and are intended to replace parts or act as additions to the multitude of models, of all kinds, now available. You can get finer scale track links for model AFVs, handrails for ships, aerials and instrument panels for aircraft, wheels for cars, scale period figures for the latter and the many kits of trucks, and there is a whole host of commercially-produced detail additives for railway modellers. The list is endless and a glance at the advert pages of leading model magazines will reveal just how much a growing industry it all is.

Within the limits of this chapter it is not possible to fully explore the whole gamut of detailing; there are too many different disciplines, and types of models within them, for a start! We can, however, discuss what is advisable and what is not. But first, we should understand that there isn't such a thing as *too* much detail.

The maxim 'if you can see it, it should be there' does hold true; just as 'if you can't see it, what's the point of adding it' also makes a lot of sense. The point is to make it as authentic as you can, within your capabilities as a modeller. But don't worry if you can't; modelling is supposed to be fun and not a 'one-upmanship' crusade, although if you intend entering competitions with your models, of necessity you will see everything in a much different light.

Detail additions fall roughly into two categories. One is to produce parts to go where the manufacturer of the kit has forgotten to put them, and two is to replace overscale parts or incorrectly shaped ones. Broadly speaking, the latter is probably the more common practice where, due to 'moulding limitations', kit parts can be dimensionally too big or simply just too crude. Examples are pitot tubes, aerials, undercarriage doors on aircraft, masts, rails, davits on ships, windscreen wipers, foot and hand controls on cars. The list is endless and it's up to the modeller to use his eyes and his own keen judgement in such cases.

Parts missed are usually confined to interior areas on aircraft, but should be added where possible, especially if they are to be visible from normal viewing angles. Small touches such as the drilling-out of gun barrels, rigging biplanes, attaching aerial wires should become part and parcel of the quest for that more detailed, in-scale look. Fine parts, for example pitot tubes on aircraft, can be, depending on scale, replaced with such things as very fine hypodermic needles or stretched sprue, just as over-thick transparencies can be replaced with thinner, and more in-scale ones plug moulded from acetate or clear plastic card, though the latter material can sometimes have a problem with clouding where smaller scale models are concerned.

Never lose sight of the fact that you can produce the necessary additives if they are not available commercially and also additives need not only be cosmetic in their use, but functional. I do not mean working parts, often referred to as 'gimmicks', but something added to serve a purpose. For example, a modeller can spend a lot of time weighting the nose of aircraft with tricycle undercarriages for an 'in scale' attitude. After all, no one wants some unscale and incorrect-looking ladder or pylon stuck up the midway point of the fuselage simply to keep the nose down.

The addition of weights, while not difficult, can often ruin the model visually, especially where an open air intake is present . . . or how about the glazed nose of a B-25 Mitchell bomber? I once read a very interesting magazine article about the latter case where the modeller stuffed lead shot in the ammunition boxes for the nose gun, in the equipment along the bombardier's station, and so on—what a chore! He would have saved himself a lot of trouble if he had simply moulded the cockpit floor in white metal! All that is needed is a silicone

A Graphy Air 1:72 scale resin conversion to Heller's Mirage III produces the IIIBE variant. Harrier range white metal ejector seats are fitted and keep the nose down. Paint chipping around the intake rims and anti-glare panel are evident.

rubber mould made of the kit part and then cast in metal. The nosewheel could also have been cast, and you don't always need RTV (Room Temperature Vulcanising) silicone rubber. I've got away with using plaster moulds for simple parts.

Jet fighters can be kept in a nose-down attitude by adding a white metal ejector seat, or recasting the kit part yourself where, at the same time, you could add a lot more detail to it before you make the mould. The point is never hesitate to replace any part with your own home-produced product if it serves the purpose of attaining a more in-scale appearance. If the part is not right, modify it or replace it and, if you can, re-mould it from your own moulds.

How to mould your own parts is not within the scope of this chapter, however, it is something that should be explored by all modellers. In the United Kingdom there are two companies who can be recommended, offering moulding rubbers, resins and metals geared to the modeller, but, most importantly in modeller's quantitites. They also offer technical advice and printed booklets on how to go about it. They are Strand Glass and Alec Tiranti (addresses at the end of this chapter).

Whatever you model, there is always scope for improvement and this is, perhaps, mirrored by the big plastic kit manufacturers with the release of 'High-Tech' kits containing white metal and etched parts. They have, at last, realised that modellers, not the toy market but *modellers*, desire something just that little bit better.

After building your model, adding the detail, and so on, it's advisable to make a base for it. A base offers protection and negates handling the model; also it can enhance the subject. Where possible fix the model to the base. You don't have to make a diorama but, especially in the case of aircraft, maximum protection is provided and stops all that carefully added detail being knocked off or damaged. Give it some thought; it's worth it.

Whether to weather?

Whether or not to weather your model is a personal thing. After lavishing great care in obtaining a superb finish why muck it all up? The simple answer is, realism! Look at any real piece of equipment or hardware very closely and you immediately realise the effects of terrain and the environment on any exposed surfaces. This will differ around the world, hot climates having a different effect to temperate ones, but the results are basically the same and it is these that we must try to emulate in miniature.

Road vehicles are notoriously susceptible to weathering. Just look at your own car, even in fine weather periods. It's all there: dust and traces of effluence from other vehicles which deposit a film on the outer surfaces. Look at the tyres: they're not matt black all over, as some modellers still insist on painting them. The tread has a different 'feel' and colour to the sidewalls and it is this, specifically, that we should try to copy in miniature.

Never go completely over the top with a weathering process, however, because what you see in 1:1 scale will not necessarily be convincing in miniature and a certain amount of artist's licence has to come into the procedure. It's the same as scale colour; it has to be applied with some forethought and restraint.

Convincing modellers to weather the finished product is another matter and, as stated earlier, it is a personal trait. Perhaps one of the best examples in favour of weathering could be found in the motion picture and film industry where, in science fiction pictures, the use of models has become, of obvious necessity, widespread. In the *Star Wars* movies the vehicles and space ship models have all received the attentions of the modelmakers' weathering sprays and brushes! Taken in context, realism has been achieved and the models, which are obviously models, look far more realistic and believable. This

The destroyer HMS *Hasty*—photographed in 1936. Light weathering streaks on the grey paintwork are evident and something ship modellers should try, to introduce a little realism to their models.

weathering was also carried out on full scale mock-ups to complete the illusion.

Weathering as a process is a technique that needs practice. New methods and 'wrinkles' crop up weekly when modellers discover more ways and means to produce effects. It can, however, be split into four broad, basic categories: an ageing process, the effects of the elements, the effects of the immediate environment of the scene depicted and effluent and stains produced by the subject itself.

The ageing process is, perhaps, the most difficult to produce convincingly, and it needs a lot of experimentation, covering everything from heavy corrosion (mainly on inanimate objects) to paint fading. Remember, you can't quickly fade paint already applied to a model; you must apply it 'faded' in the first place.

Effects of the elements break down basically to rain streaks, deposits of snow and ice, mud, dust, rust, abrasions such as stone chips on road vehicles and aircraft operating from rough strips. Try sitting down and compiling a list and you'll be amazed at what you come up with.

The immediate environment is totally different from the others and would mainly concern the diorama builder, where the process has more meaning on the overall effect of the model. For example, if an armoured vehicle or suchlike had just demolished a house it would be covered by not only bits of the building, but by a lot of dust caused by the demolition. If the vehicle was only in the vicinity, it would still have received 'treatment' from the action. Any vehicle depicted emerging

Accurate Armour's 1:35 scale Cromwell complete with a Verlinden turret crew. The vehicle has been weathered with powders after drybrushing to highlight the details. Note the camouflage net on the turret rear which is from an armour accessories range. The vehicle needs extra stowage and is a little "too clean" at this stage.

from water would have its previously immersed parts show up as a glossy wet finish in the majority of cases. Surface paint chipped by such actions is worth considering too. Simple, yes, but it's surprising how these very obvious touches are ignored by some modellers.

Stains and other marks that emanate from 'machinery' are the most commonly applied weathering techniques and usually the most abused. Powder stains from guns, exhaust efflux, oil leaks are common on military aircraft, even modern ones! I've rarely seen a pristine combat aircraft. And who has seen a sparkling truck on the roads? Granted the cab upper area may be 'clean,' but what about the rest? Diesel railway locomotives stay really 'clean' for a very short time and electric locomotives are not far behind. Dirt soon appears from exhausts and cooling fan grilles over the roof and especially areas just above the bogies.

Weathering a model can be done in many ways, but it is usually done with paint, either dry-brushed or airbrushed, or alternatively with powders marketed specially for the task, or chalk pastels ground down to powder form. Combination of both mediums will cover most eventualities.

Paint

Using paint for weathering purposes can, with care, be most realistic. Applied by airbrush, convincing stains (if the airbrush has a fine jet) are possible and some modellers can produce different 'shades' of metal on natural finish aircraft by careful masking processes. This works well on larger scale models though the effect can be overpowering, to say the least, in the smaller scales. If you are adept at using the airbrush you should find very little difficulty in using it for such purposes.

Dry-brushing is a modelling technique everyone should try to master because it can produce some excellent effects. The idea is to use a brush dipped in paint and then all the paint wiped from the bristles. Next wipe the brush, to and fro, on paper to remove any remaining excess, leaving just a hint of colour remaining. Lightly flick the bristles over the model where the raised detail will benefit from a slight paint deposit. This technique needs practice and it's advisable to experiment on an old model.

Another technique used which acts as the basis for a weathered finish is to paint the model from dark to light tones. This method works especially well on armoured vehicles and, after the first coat of paint, will lighten all succeeding coats. The effect is to emphasise raised detail and panel areas which can be further enhanced with overall washes of very thin matt black and dark grey paint, and dry-brushing to finish. Although a painting technique, it effectively gives the model a weathered look.

Powders

Although not apparently suited to model aircraft, they do have their uses. Powders are a superb medium for road vehicles and military vehicles—especially tanks, ships, buildings, railway locomotives and stock.

Powdering chalk pastels for weathering—simply rub them on glass paper, produce the dust and apply with a brush.

Powders are marketed commercially and, perhaps, the best-known range in the UK come from Carr's Modelling Products. These are finely ground powders, slightly 'waxy in consistency which aids adhesion, and available in many different and most suitable colours. They can be applied with a brush and the boon is that if mistakes are made the powder can be removed quite easily. For permanence, a fixative spray is advised, though if the model is not to be handled it's not really necessary. The powders can be mixed with clear acrylic mediums, gloss, satin or matt, for different effects; one example would be rust streaks on a ship's hull, from scupper and hawse-holes.

An alternative powder can be produced by rubbing chalk-type artists' pastels on glass paper to produce a small pile of dust. This is then transferred to the model by brush and does need a fixative spray for permanence. The grains are usually coarser, but this can work in the modellers' favour where, bound with acrylic medium, a form of dried powdery mud can be produced. Powders deserve the modellers' attention and experimentation is advised, and it does bring rewards.

Following are some typical, yet basic efforts pertaining to models which will give a more realistic overall appearance.

Careful study of these British Matildas will give a lot of ideas for weathering an armoured vehicle. Note the oil streaks on the side plates.

Desert dust has gathered on the raised ribs on the side of this *Kübelwagen* contrasting with the vehicle's dark grey colour. Weathering powders, carefully applied can produce this effect.

Mud, dirt and dust

Mud, a feature beloved of tank modellers, is easily overdone and thus can become totally unrealistic. It is one of the disciplines best played down. Thick mud deposits can be represented with small amounts of body putty, spackling paste with powder added to remove the 'smooth' texture, or epoxy putty such as Milliput. If the mud is to be newly picked up and, thus, wet in appearance this must be represented by the careful application of gloss varnish.

For dry dirt and dust look no further than weathering powders, which, when carefully applied, can impart a most realistic finish, even on small scale figurines. One point: domestic dust picked up by models should be discouraged as unrealistic. It photographs very badly on small scale models, coming up in the photo as pebbles. It is, after all, mainly flakes of human skin! Also, do not use soil from the garden, but do sift the dry dust you find in the gutter, as this can be used for many effects.

Finally, a warning. Do not use any dusts found by sanding polyester or polyurethane resins. These are very harmful if ingested in great quantities and, should you happen to build a polyurethane resin kit which needs the parts sanding, do it outside, not in a confined space and keep the glass paper wet – and do wear a face mask.

Rust

Again, weathering powders are very good for representing heavy corrosion. Depending on the scale of the model, a combination of varnishes and powders can produce the result required.

Rust varies in colour too from straw colours to orange and this also, of course, depends on the type of metal that has corroded. Use acrylic matt varnish mixed with a spot of paint and a little rust-coloured powder added, if heavy corrosion is desired, and paint this directly onto the model in the appropriate areas, heeding the fact that rust doesn't just form anywhere. There has to be a reason for its presence, so think before you apply it. When the streak or stain is dry you can dry-brush it if you have added powder to highlight it and give it some depth for effect!

Exhaust stains

After using the airbrush and a conventional brush for many years to produce exhaust stains I've settled exclusively upon powders for making them. A most common example is the stain from the exhaust outlet on a piston-engined aircraft. These stains when carried out in a subtle manner can greatly enhance the overall appearance of the model.

The powder is lightly applied in a 'scrubbing' action where the efflux would stain the paint work or natural metal. Don't overdo it because in miniature it doesn't ring quite true if you produce thick, solid black stains. I am aware of the huge stains caused by leaded petrol on British aircraft of WW2, but even this doesn't look convincing in model form and it usually leads to explanations having to be given which also defeats the object. The viewer must immediately *know* that the stain you have put on your model is an exhaust stain.

AFVs and some other road vehicles are exactly the opposite, however—thick oily exhaust fumes leaving thick black dirty

An RAF Mustang shows "classic" exhaust stains, the most commonly applied 'mark' on model piston-engined aeroplanes. Note the radio mast with wires—a good detail to add.

Not only propeller driven aircraft are stained. Note the gas wash around the ports on the nose-mounted M61 A1 20mm cannon of this Canadian F-18 Hornet.

stains in the vicinity of the exhaust outlet pipes, the diesel engines of the Soviet heavy tanks of WW2 being notorious for this. Work these stains from light to dark, using thinned paint and increasing the frequency of the colour until your eye tells you to stop and you achieve the desired result. Exhaust stains are nearly always flat black but, as always, there will be exceptions to the rule. Vehicles, unlike aircraft, do not have a slipstream to blow away exhaust effluent, so it collects in thicker and much darker patches.

Powder stains

The simulated effects of powder 'wash' from guns on aircraft models is, perhaps, the most commonly 'overdone' weathering feature of all. Again, use powders to good effect here, and be sparing in their application, avoiding heavy soot-like deposits; remember it should be only a surface film on aircraft. Shell case ejection ports, too, are victims of over-emphasis of staining when only a thin streak is needed; most of the expanding gases of a gun go out of the muzzle not the ejection opening.

Tank guns normally only show staining around the muzzle, or muzzle brake if one is fitted. Paint is also burnt away here with prolonged firing, the muzzle flash accounting for this and any smoke residue for the powder staining.

Hits on vehicles sometimes show scorch or flash marks coming up as black stains around the point of entry. Such battle damage deserves careful photographic study if you are to be at all realistic.

Revival's Ferrari 500—a metal and plastic kit with vinyl tyres. Subtle dry-brushing on various parts, especially the tyre treads, gives a more realistic finish.

Tyres

The tread on tyres can be dry-brushed to give a good cosmetic effect on the model and give added depth to something that many simply paint as matt black and leave as finished. Even a newly-fitted tyre after one revolution will pick up dust from the ground, rendering the tread a lighter colour than the rest. This should be reproduced in miniature and can be done even on the vinyl tyres some manufacturers are including in their kits. It works especially well on aircraft tyres, even those with no tread, where the area of the tyre in contact with the ground should be lightened in contrast to the sidewalls.

Begin with dark grey working progressively lighter until the desired shade is reached. Do not make it too light and, if the

Close-up of the running gear of a King Tiger, complete with grease stains issuing from the hubs—a commonly modelled feature, but often overdone.

tyre is vinyl, lightly sand the surface before you paint it. If the tread is prominent, after you have weathered it, dry-brush it lightly with an even lighter shade to pick up the detail.

Oil stains

Piston engined aircraft are notorious for leaking oil over the airframe which, in model form, can realistically improve what the modeller is trying to convey. Again, it's a feature that should not be overdone and its visual effect kept to a minimum, even on tanks and suchlike.

Oil leaking from a worn engine has lots of carbon in it and is near black in colour, but lubricating oils are usually greenish-brown in colour. On deciding what you want, acrylic satin varnish with streaks of the appropriate colour added makes a good representation of oil streaking. The streak will be darker at the point of exit and grow fainter towards the end of the flow as the oil thins out—a minor point but it's surprising how many don't follow this simple observation.

Chipped paintwork

Wherever humans walk or handle parts of machinery a certain amount of 'wear' is evident. Leaving aside the effects of the elements on paintwork, handles, steps, and snap fasteners on aircraft, the treatment of the paintwork should indicate that the model is not one solid mass, but made up from a lot of individual removable panels. Always play down this effect. It's well known that some Japanese WW2 aircraft didn't keep their

Gull Models 1:48 scale vacform kit of the Japanese Tachikawa Ki-36 "Ida" shows chipped green paintwork revealing the natural aluminium underneath.

dark green paint jobs for long and great flakes of the stuff peeled off, but representing this in model form doesn't seem real at all no matter how you try.

Bare metal showing through where paint is scuffed and worn away, such as on AFVs, is an ideal weathering feature to make on the model and very easy to do. Never use bright silver paint, it just does not look authentic. Use gunmetal, or mix a little silver with a lot of dark blue to get the effect. Apply the paint very sparingly with the brush and, when dry, mix up a slightly lighter shade and highlight the area. The technique needs practice, but once mastered, the effects possible really bring the appearance of a model to life.

On larger scale models, the first coat of paint could be an overall metallic and this could be allowed to show through with careful masking as the successive top coats are applied.

If this chapter inspires anyone to take a good hard look at their models and makes them wonder if they could improve them in any way by the addition of details, or by weathering for a more realistic appearance, then I have been successful. If, however, the simple techniques mentioned are not for you, then so be it, so long as you obtain satisfaction from your hobby.

Next time you attend a model competition compare the models 'straight from the box' to those where the modeller has added detail and weathered the finish. The difference may not be remarkable at first glance, but, personal taste aside, there' no getting away from which is the more realistic!

Useful addresses

Carrs Modelling Products, Unit 5, Centre 88, Elm Grove, Wimbledon, London SW19 4HE.
Strand Glassfibre Ltd, Brentway Trading Estate, Brentford, Middlesex TW8 8ER.
Alec Tiranti, 70 High Street, Theale, Reading, Berks RG7 5AR.

9 CARS

MAT IRVINE

The first commercially produced car kits using the modern injection process came from the Gowland and Gowland company and were to 1 : 32 scale. This scale emerged purely by chance, as half of 1 : 16 scale which was then being used for their original 'toy' model cars. However, since then, although 1 : 32 scale is still used by some model manufacturers, by far and away the majority of model car kits come in either 1 : 25 or 1 : 24 scale, the former being the older and still used by most of the American car kit companies still in production. These are, AMT, Jo-Han, MPC and Revell. The remaining US major car company, Monogram, uses 1 : 24 scale which is also used by the rest of the model manufacturers in Europe and Japan.

Europe and Japan

There is obviously a difference between these scales, particularly noticeable if one compares like vehicles, say

Some of the earliest injected polystyrene model car kits. The top kit, from Gowland and Gowland, used generic box-art for their series, while the issues from the early Revell company could boast of individual artwork.

Monogram's 1 : 24 1936 Ford against AMT's 1 : 25 scale version. For most collectors, however, this difference is negligible and most will collect examples of the two scales alongside each other. The first car kits in 1 : 25 scale came from Revell, as an offshoot to their co-production of the 1 : 32 scale Gowland and Gowland series, and from AMT and Jo-Han who started by producing 'promo' car models for the full-size car manufacturers. 'Promos'—short for 'promotional'— used to be produced for all the 1 : 1 scale cars, invariably as friction-drive giveaways, and although the widespread distribution of promos has declined, some specialist issues are still produced of old cars from the Jo-Han range, through their X–EL division, and of new cars under the MPC logo through their new owners, The ERTL Company.

These early promos, although having a semi-scale chassis and no engine, had extremely good body detail and it was not long before AMT and Jo-Han began to sell them in disassembled form as construction kits proper. From here, it was hardly a great step to add more detail, such as opening hoods, engines and custom options. The early Revell kits went a slightly different route, having multi-piece bodies, although very soon, Revell adopted the now standard one-piece body for model car construction.

Other companies joined the car kit production, and some, such as Monogram, are still in production with their 1 : 24, 1 : 32 and giant 1 : 8 scale ranges. Other names, such as Aurora in 1 : 24 scale, Eldon, IMC and Hawk in 1 : 24 scale and Pyro in 1 : 32 scales have disappeared, although most of their tooling

The first model car scale was 1:32, and although it has in many ways been overtaken by the larger 1:24 or 1:25 scales, it still has its enthusiasts. Some of the earliest examples have seen the light of day again under Airfix's new owners, Humbrol.

1:43 scale is supposed to have come about as a model scale as it is the nearest to '0' gauge. It is mostly used for diecast models, but there have been a few examples in plastic, particularly the Heller series.

was acquired by other companies and some of the kits reissued. In Britain, Airfix began their car kit production in 1:32 scale very early on in their existence. Later they issued a few in 1:24 scale and reissued a number from MPC, but these were in 1:25 scale. When the Frog company existed, they made several in 1:16 scale, while more recently, Matchbox began car kit production, but stayed with 1:32 scale.

In Europe, Heller, ESCI and Italeri use 1:24 scale, though Heller uses 1:8, 1:16 1:32 and 1:43 scales also. When Japan started car kit production, they too used 1:24 scale, but other odd scales can also occur, such as 1:20 and even 1:28!

Over the years motor car kits have dominated the scene although other types of vehicles have surfaced from trucks in 1:24/5 and 1:32 scales plus motorbikes in several larger scales. Even push-bikes and snowmobiles have occasionally appeared.

Construction breakdown

Most modern car kits use similar construction methods, whatever the scale, with the main bodywork being moulded in a single piece. In most cases, the bonnet is tooled separately as there is engine detail included, and sometimes the boot and doors are also operable. The chassis will range from a single

Car kits have become more and more complex. Fujimi's 'Enthusiast Series' are probably the top of the range and this Ferrari 288 can boast of an engine of over 70 separate parts.

piece, as used by the old promo-type kits, with holes designed to take metal rod axles, to types where the front and rear axles and exhaust systems are separate, and to the most advanced, where the complete suspension is supplied as separate parts.

Similarly, engines can come as a simple 'two halves' type with few additional parts, to some incredible detailed offerings with up to seventy individual parts for the engines alone!

Interiors are usually a single moulding for the basic shape, again an off-shoot of the promo kits, though separate seats, instrument panels and steering wheel are normal. More advanced kits will break these parts down into yet more, and many kits will also provide custom or competition parts. Decals for the instrument dials and radio are becoming more common as are separate seat belts, especially in many Japanese kits. Clear parts are usually included, if only for the windscreen glass. Modern kits will have clear parts for head and tail lamps as well, although some older US kits will probably still have the headlamps moulded as part of the grille and bumper. However, these kits invariably have the tail lamps moulded in translucent red, which saves additional painting.

A 'chromed' runner is almost always included with most car kits of any scale, although the terminology should really be 'vacuum-plated'. This process can also be used to produce 'brass' parts for some vintage cars, and some modern customs. Lastly, most car kits contain what are usually called 'rubber' tyres, although the material is actually vinyl. A few kits have the wheels and tyres moulded integrally, usually in two halves, in conventional polystyrene.

In recent years, and particularly from the Japanese kit

companies, there has been a growing tendency to issue 'multi-material' car kits where white-metal and etched parts are included along with the plastic.

Preparation

Most car kits can be broken down into four construction sections—the body, interior, engine and chassis. Obviously there will be differences—there may not be an engine for example, but overall, most of these preparation points will be relevant to nearly all kits of any scale.

The first point is the fairly obvious one of reading the instruction sheet. However, this isn't to say that the instructions will be the only way a kit can be built because experience will tell you your own particular way of dealing with each company's product. Usually the four sub-assemblies can be dealt with separately, only being brought together at the end for final completion. It is not unusual though to find—especially with say, mid-engined sports car—that the engine has to be assembled into the body at a very early stage, so again it's down to thoroughly checking the instructions first.

Having made the initial checks that all the parts are in fact there, and there are no serious faults, the various parts for the sub-assemblies can be separated out. As with any kit, some parts are best assembled before painting, others are best left on the runner and painted first. It is also advisable to decide early on if the kit provides options which you are going to incorporate. Most US car kits provide 'custom' or 'racing' options which can effect the basic assembly.

Many of the Japanese sports car kits provide several versions in one kit, so you have to make up your mind at the beginning just which version to build. Others will give options on the basic car, such as whether pop-up headlamps are assembled up or down, whether you want a left or right-hand drive, or a manual or automatic gearbox. Others provide common runners to several kits and, although most plans give a diagram indicating which parts are not used, it can still lead to confusion if the optional parts are similar in shape.

Occasionaly you may find sink-marks on some of the larger parts. One-piece car bodies can be prone to this where locating pins, or lugs, are also provided under the bonnet and boot. However, they are easily filled with a good modelling putty, sanded and primed before the main painting.

Painting

Any model is dependent on its final finish, and here a few basic points which, followed at the beginning will mean less problems later on. Some kits come with a plastic finish that almost doesn't require paint. Although this may have certain merits it cannot really be recommended, as any plastic will look just that—plastic—without any additional work. Consequently, if car models are going to be painted they are most likely to receive a spray finish. This can be done in two ways, either with an airbrush (spray-gun) or from a commercial aerosol can. As far as the latter is concerned there are options, for although the major model paint manufacturers make spray paint especially formulated for kits, it is quite feasible to use other types, although several precautions are necessary.

As far as the model companies are concerned, most of the sprays in the western world come from Humbrol and Revell in Britain and Europe, and Testors and Pactra in the USA. All four produce a wide range of colours in several different types of finishes. The most popular are solid gloss colours which form the backbone of any range of colours, along with metallics. Revell have, in fact, specially formulated a range of Car Metallics which compliment the type of finish being used on full-size cars, especially those of European origin.

The American ranges, however, also include two types not available in Europe, although they are mentioned here to complete the descriptions. These are termed Metalflakes and Candies. Metalflake is, as its name suggests, a more striking version of metallic and, the paint for the full-size cars actually has tiny flakes of metal mixed in with the pigment. Conse-

Gunze Sangyo pioneered the multi-material kit using not only polystyrene parts, but white-metal, photo-etched, vinyl and an assortment of tubing and wiring. This Ferrari GTO has a white-metal chassis and makes a good transition from the total plastic car kit to the totally metal.

quently it requires special mixing and applying. It does, however, provide a very 'deep' glittering type of finish, most suitable for custom cars. Candies (sometimes termed 'Kandies') have a similar use in that, unlike a pigmented paint, they contain a dye. This means the more coats that are applied, the deeper the colour. Also, the type of base coat it is applied over will dictate the overall shade. Their development was designed for the type of radical custom car coming out of California in the 60s, but they can also be very effective on a car built purely stock.

Although the Testors and Pactra range are not generally available in the UK, there are options. Many touch-up sprays for full-size cars can be used on models—as long as the body is well primed first. Most of these 'full-size' paints are a different formula to model paints, and most will effect the surface of the plastic if used direct. One range from Pactra though, that has been available in Britain, is their paint designed for the clear 'Lexan' racing bodies used on radio-controlled cars. This paint is also suitable for 'static' car models, provided the bodies are well primed, as before. This range only includes gloss and metallics, but there are different shades to those available from Humbrol and Revell. They will require a thorough coating of gloss varnish as they tend to dry matt.

An airbrush will, of course, allow any paint to be applied that is available in a tinlet and, if a special colour is needed that isn't available as a commercial spray, this is really the only option. An airbrush will also allow some of the more exotic designs to be painted onto a car body to match the full-size originals. Parts to be spray painted will need support and, especially with one-piece car bodies, the easiest method is to utilize an old wire coat hanger, bent to shape. Invariably it will be self-supporting inside the body shell, though occasionally, double-sided tape will be needed to hold it in place. If you have one of the older annual kits from AMT or Jo-Han, these used mounting posts under the bodyshell, which are very convenient to attach a wire holder to.

Priming the parts is also a very important stage when painting a car body, especially so if additional parts have been added before the painting, or if any filler has been used. All the established model paint manufacturers have a primer in their range, and the base colour of this primer can sometimes effect the top coat. Candy paints are an example, as the top coat, being transparent, will reveal the base coat. However, some metallics will also change their overall appearance depending on the base colour. Revell's Car Metallics work particularly well over a black undercoat as it makes them appear 'deeper' in texture. Sometimes it can be advantageous, if you are using the same metallic colour for interior and exterior, to use the exterior over matt black and the interior over matt white. The latter will then appear a lighter shade of the exterior, more suitable for metallic fabrics.

Spray painting—whether from a commercial can or an airbrush—is an art in its own right and, if you have not attempted any spray finishes before, you are well advised to practice on scrap material beforehand. The basic rule when spraying a whole surface (such as a car body) is never to start and stop actually over the spraying area, always begin the paint spray before you reach the model, and continue it after.

Build up the layers one at a time; a number of light passes are far better than one or two heavy coats as the paint will invariably run. There is merit in applying the final coat of a gloss finish 'wet' (i.e. fairly thick) to give the glossiest finish, but this too will come with practice. Most model paints will dry to a set sheen, regardless of how they've been applied. In general, modern model spray paints are extremely well formulated and, with the few basic rules mentioned, are very forgiving and will give good results, even for a newcomer.

The spray cans themselves should be shaken well before use—all (bar gloss varnishes) have an agitator inside—to assist with the mixing. They also benefit from warming before spraying by standing the can in a bowl of hand-hot (only) water. After use, invert the can and spray a quick burst to clear the nozzle. This isn't a waste of paint as otherwise you'll probably find the whole can becomes unusable.

The painted model should be left somewhere where it will not come into contact with a lot of flying dust. A proper drying cabinet is probably not part of most people's modelling paraphernalia, but a large box with suitable hanging attachments should not be beyond the capability of most modellers.

With regard to the other, smaller parts of the kit, a number are best painted *in situ* on the runner. Others can be part-assembled—engine blocks, rear axles etc.—before painting. Alternatively it can be advantageous to collect all the parts that will be the same colour together, and then spray them. This can save considerable time, especially when it comes to, say, painting fiddly suspension components. The exact method of this will depend on the layout of the kit's parts. You may be lucky and find that all the parts are on the same runner, in which case remove the parts that won't be this colour (still attached to their direct runner) for painting separately. Then the whole runner can basically be sprayed the one colour.

It will probably be more likely that the parts you want the same colour will be on different runners, in which case each can be removed, again attached to part of the runner for support, and collected together. Clothes pegs are a cheap and useful method of holding small parts for painting, and the wooden ones are better than the plastic ones!

Colours

These will obviously, in the main, be up to the individual builder. However, a few points can be generalised. Stock engine blocks are usually some basic primary colour—red, orange, blue, green or even black. Where the block is aluminium, or a similar compound, such as with modern sports cars, the colour is usually just this—aluminium. Even if the main block has a colour, the gearbox can be silver or aluminium.

For a full custom finish for your engine, chrome is not unusual, but in most cases the plated parts can be painted gunmetal or aluminium. The only exception here is the rocker

Variations on a theme. Monogram, not normally known for making 'annual' cars did issue the 1986 Chevrolet Monte Carlo and the 1988 Buick Grand National, which although based on the same GM body-style, exhibited some considerable differences.

covers which are invariably chromed. Carburettors, however, are rarely chromed, nor are aircleaners or alternators, all of which usually appear on the plated runner. Carburettors are best painted aluminium while the modern alternator can be aluminium for the pulley and orange for the main body. Stock aircleaners are a primary colour or black. A safe colour for all distributors is black, though orange is fairly common for the top part at least.

Period batteries are always black, with coloured caps. Modern batteries appear in almost all shades, though white is probably the most common, with the sealed lid being a contrasting colour. Radiators are almost always painted black for, even if this isn't the original colour, they always seem to end up this way! The header tank can be silver, aluminium or even a bronze shade. If it's a modern car with a separate header tank, these are usually plastic and translucent white. The same colour can be applied to washer bottles where fitted.

Moving further under the car, the prop shafts are nearly always black or 'metallic' (assuming a front engine—rear drive set up), though the universal joints (if detailed) can be picked out in a contrasting shade. The rear axle is usually a similar colour, although some appear in red primer which can make a change. Front axles and steering assemblies are probably best generalised as 'black' or 'metallic', unless otherwise stated. If shock absorbers are visible, the thicker part of the body is usually some bright colour, red or blue, with the piston part either silver, or perhaps more realisticaly black, (due to the effects of the environment!).

Springs of all types, leaf or coil, can be black or metallic. Where a coil spring is moulded 'solid' (as is usually the case), paint the interior matt black and then carefully go round the spring itself with aluminium or even silver. Fuel tanks are usually unpainted i.e. they are rusty! Metallic should match a pristine tank or black if it has been undercoated. Similarly, exhaust systems are the first items to rust (unless they are stainless steel) and can be either new (aluminium), or old (a reddish metallic). This colour also works well for the exhaust manifolds themselves, being cast iron. Specialist exhaust 'headers' on American customs and racers are often white.

The basic underside of the car can prove a problem for, if it is meant to have been undercoated, everything will virtually be black, making for a quick, but somewhat uninteresting finish. On some cars, usually sports types, the underbody panels are the colour of the bodywork, in which case the running gear will stand out anyway. Alternatively, use black as the basic floor panel colour and add the additional details. A dark grey can also look effective as the background colour.

Note that these details can also apply to the solid 'one-piece' chassis found in the older 'annual' releases from AMT, Jo-Han or MPC, where suspension, prop-shaft and axles are moulded as one; sometimes the engine pans as well. However, there is a great deal of detailing that can be done here with careful painting, and a one-peice chassis can be made to look just as effective as one with many separate parts.

Stock kits

Even without adding detailing, paying attention to two areas of an average car kit can make it stand out and take on an air of reality. One area is the grille and headlamps while the other is the wheels and tyres. A large number of car kits arrive with a one-piece plated front grille and bumper. This is a throwback to the original promo kits and invariably applies to American machinery more than others. Using the part as it is will mean all the detail disappearing into the glare of the chrome. By looking at an example of a full-size car with a reasonable amount of chrome on the front end (admittedly getting more difficult these days with modern cars!) will reveal that by no means is the whole area 'chromed'.

The first stage is to fill in all the recesses of the grille with a thin wash of matt black paint. This should be thin enough so that it will flow over the raised areas, but still retain a feel of 'blackness' when in the recesses. Any overspill can be wiped off with a clean cloth moistened with thinners afterwards. The whole of the front bumper may not all be chromed; look out for

The classic American car model. This is Revell's 1954 Chevrolet featuring opening hood, trunk and doors and steerable wheels.

171

where rubber inserts on over-riders can be painted semi-gloss black.

With these types of kits the headlamps may also be incorporated into the same part and headlamps definitely do not appear chromed as such. The best way to represent what is, after all, clear glass over a chromed reflector, is a 50:50 mix of matt white and silver. This mix can also be used for reversing lamps.

Wheels and tyres can also be detailed straight from the stock kit. A well known tip is to sand the tyres to make the look 'used' This idea probably began life in the early 60s with drag-racing slicks which definitely do need sanding to make them authentic, but it can apply to any vinyl tyre. It is simplicity itself and all it requires is a reasonably coarse glass paper. Hold the tyre carefully (ensuring you don't sand your finger tips as well!) and go round the circumference of the tyre removing the outer surface. This can also remove a moulding line which is occasionaly visible on some model tyres.

There is also a type of tyre being used in some kits that comes in two halves, though is still moulded in vinyl rather than a polystyrene. This is actually the worst type to deal with for it appears to be impervious to cementing. However, with care, super glue can work. Alternatively, use a contact adhesive. Once dry, this type of tyre definitely benefits from the sanding process.

Further details can be applied to the sides of the tyre where appropiate, with either white-walls—popular for the resurgence of interest with US cars of the 50s and 60s—and the picking out in white of the lettering, particularly on drag slicks. Both additions require a fine eye and brush and although normal modelling enamel paint can be used, because the tyre is flexible, it can crack off. Some of the acryllics appear to work better here, although if the tyre is not subjected to stress, which means assembling the wheel into the tyre before painting, enamels can work perfectly well.

Attention can also be paid to the wheel itself, particularly if it is a chromed type with recesses. The same process of a thin wash of matt black, as used on the grilles, can be applied to make the detail stand out. Some wheels, such as American 'mags' (magnesium) are spoked, making the backing plate, or brake drum, show through the holes. A neat detailing point here is to paint this inner surface a contrasting colour, say bright red, to make it show through the wheel itself.

Modern European and Japanese cars mostly have non-chromed wheels or, more likely, wheel covers, some of which are painted the same as the body or a contrasting colour. These can also be 'handed' i.e. they are designed for either the left or right-hand side of the car. For wire spoked wheels, a favourite of early sports cars, model manufacturers vary from producing a single moulding, to highly detailed multi-piece wheel halves in either plastic, or etched metal. The wheel halves really need no other attention except care in assembly; for wire spoked wheels, use a wash of matt black.

Rear lamps and indicators

The original car kits, especially those in 1:24 or 1:25 scales, nearly always contained translucent red parts for the rear lamps. As these were almost exclusively American cars, which do not require amber indicators (although they are changing over), they worked very well. Translucent red parts are still provided in some kits, mainly those from the American 'big five'—AMT, Jo-Han, Monogram, MPC and Revell, but with the growth of European and Japanese subjects as car kits, more and more rear and indicator lenses were being mouded in clear plastic. The original method of colouring them was to simply paint them red or orange, either the whole part or just on the back. Both methods had disadvantages and what was needed was translucent paint to correctly match the plastic lens of the full-size car. In more recent years, some of the paint companies have provided these, with both US manufacturers and Tamiya providing the main source for the UK. The Tamiya range of paints is acryllic (water based) and six are made in a transparent dye including red and orange. Now it's an easy matter to paint the whole of the rear lamp assemblies the appropriate shades, adding front and side indicators where necessary. Where a plated front grille contains built-in indicators, the Tamiya paint is better than the solid colour, as it still allows the 'chrome' to show through as a reflector.

The Tamiya translucent paints can also be used to tint other clear parts, such as the window glass itself or the bug screens as found on many American pick-ups. The paint can, in fact, be airbrushed, although use meths as a thinner, not water. They can also be used to build up a form of 'candy' finish, where actual cans of this paint are not available. However, it does dry matt and will require a gloss varnish coat to finish.

Interiors

The interior colour of a vehicle should not clash too violently with its exterior. Perhaps this applies more to stock cars than to a radical custom, but even with the latter, taste should at least form part of the overall plans. Some model car companies are even listing stock finishes—interior and exterior—for their new and reissued kits; AMT and Tamiya are two examples.

Interiors are rarely one overall colour and, even if they are, different materials take on different shades. Black is a favourite interior colour, especially for sports cars, although here using mixes of even the standard tinlet blacks—matt, semi-gloss/satin and gloss—will give a far better result than painting it all matt black. The seats would most likely be satin finished black, particularly if they are leather. Dry-brushing a grey carefully over the top will simulate an authentic leather-type of wear. Floors and side panels will more likely be matt black, but certain areas—ashtrays, map pockets etc, could be picked out in satin. Instrument panels are usually semi-gloss whether they be leather or plastic, though watch out where there could be wood or chrome inserts.

Instrument dials are tricky to deal with effectively, although there is a definite growth of providing these with decals, particularly from European and Japanese kit manufacturers. Sometimes the dials are individual items on the sheet, which are the most difficult to apply as some are only an ⅛ in. diameter! More and more though, the whole panel comes as

Even with showroom cars, interior details can sometimes be quite exotic. This Tamiya Toyota gives the builder separate decals for each seat.

one decal which obviously makes things far easier. Some kits even have a 'reversed' decal that is applied on clear 'glass' to act as the front of the dials and a few Japanese car kits even contain alternative 'analogue' or 'digital' instrument displays, depending on your taste!

Other decals can also be supplied for the interior depending on the car. Some, like Ferraris, usually have a badge for the centre of the steering wheel, while if it's a racing or rally car, there will usually be markings for the obligatory fire extinguisher and, sometimes, the seat harness as well.

In the original days of the promo car kits from the US, a moulded lap-type belt was supplied, which can still be found in the various reissues from AMT and Jo-Han. Now the trend is to give the modeller the buckles and fittings as injection or etched metal parts, and seat belt material to build yourself. Hasegawa have used this method with their car kits and Fujimi also provide parts to built your own belts, though the belt material itself is cut from the instruction sheet.

It's interesting to note that the model car kits are attempting to keep pace with their full-size counterparts and, with the introduction of the 1988 Annual releases from MPC, most contain cellular phones and aerials.

Special paint finishes and decal application
Two-tone paint schemes are found on many full-size cars and can make a change for the model builder. Generally this should not cause any more problems than a single colour finish, if certain rules are followed. As a very general rule, the lightest colour should be applied first over a primed body. Any doors, hood or trunk lids should be taped in position if the colour goes over them, and any roll pans, spoilers etc, should also be applied unless there will be a problem of getting a good paint finish underneath, say, a trunk-mounted spoiler, in which case it will have to be painted separately.

The first colour should then be allowed to dry thoroughly—and this will usually take up to a week. Model paint initially dries very fast, but takes several days (or even weeks) to reach its maximum hardness. Once you are convinced that it is thoroughly dry, the line of the masking can be worked out. The correct masking tape is definitely best here as some types of tape will not give a fine enough edge. As an additional tip, the tape should be laid out on a sheet of glass and, with a steel rule as an edge, a fresh line cut to ensure that it is as sharp as possible. This is then used as the line of the second colour and pressed well down on its edge to ensure there is no seepage of paint underneath. If the line you are masking is less than the width of the tape, the one piece will be sufficient and it can be cut carefully along the other edge with a sharp modelling knife. If the area is larger than a single width of tape it can either be built up from several more lengths of tape or some other material.

Paper is not advisable unless it is of the waxed type, as paint can seep through. A polythene bag, suitably cut, would be better. It is also advisable to pack the inside of the car body with wadding of some type (paper can be used here, such as kitchen towel) to prevent any overspray getting out through the windows (this only really applies to a model where the top half is the lighter colour, though aesthetically this is usually the case.)

When the last coat of paint has been applied and before it is completely dry, remove the tape. This will prevent the edge tearing between the first and second colours for, with the paint still being tacky, it will 'mould' itself along the edge. If the masking has been done correctly there should not be any seepage of colour, but even in the best prepared cases this can happen. All is not lost, however, as before the paint has completely dried, the excess can usually be carefully removed with clean kitchen towel, moistened with fresh thinners, using a clean part for every wipe (otherwise you'll transfer the removed paint back onto the model!). This is another reason why the first paint colour has to be thoroughly dry before the second is applied.

Reissuing kits as a set has always been popular with maufacturers as it maximises the use of the tooling. These three Indianapolis 500 Pace Cars were originally issued by AMT as individual kits, but have recently been reissued by their new partner, MPC, as a set.

If a third (or more) colour is required, the whole process is repeated and, once the total required colours are on the model, any final touching up to the lines can be done with a fine paintbrush and a small amount of the actual spray paint, sprayed into a handy container (usually the spray can lid).

If you require the colours to blend or feather into one another there are several methods. The most straightforward is to cut a rough mask from card and to stand it over the model, or attach it to the wire holder if this is being used. The closer the card mask, the finer the line and vice versa. A more accurate method is to mask with tape as before, but to leave the edge of the tape away from the body, basically by the amount of feathering required. For example if the edge of the tape is bent up by only 1 mm/$\frac{1}{16}$ in. the feathering line will be very fine. If it is 12 mm/$\frac{1}{2}$ in. there will obviously be a much greater division and a wider edge. If finer detailing is required the only real answer is to use an airbrush.

Decal application can vary considerably from none at all on the outside of a car body, to pin-stripe lining, up to a full coverage most often seen with American stock car racing or rally cars. It should be unnecessary to say that it is vital to ensure that the paint surface is completely dry before attempting any decal application, especially where there is a complex scheme—water and half-dried paint do not mix! Most decals benefit from being carefully cut out from their surround to ensure there is no edge of clear decal left. This is obviously

Even the most radical of machinery sometimes needs repair—here Revell's J-2000 Pro-Street Pontiac, uses some of the tools from the Fujimi set.

more practical in some cases than others and common sense will tell you which applies. Decals also benefit from the use of a special setting agent, whether or not it is being applied over a complex curved surface, as it helps with the seating of the decal, even on a flat surface, and can prevent 'silvering' (where air is trapped under the decal). Decals should only be applied to a gloss surface, so here cars have a slight advantage over aircraft and AFVs.

Always work with one subject at a time, or a logical set if they have to be matched. Some of the most exotic schemes, invariably on racing machinery, have to be applied in a special order. Hasegawa's Porsche 944, for example, has up to four layers of decals to be applied which all have to go on in the correct order—and be allowed to dry in between applications. It is becoming more usual to provide markings for all parts of the car, so as well as the bodywork, additional decals for the front and rear glass, wheel discs and even in the engine compartment can be included. Excess water can be carefully blotted away, though if a setting agent has been used, this will seat the decal correctly and it should be left to dry on its own.

It won't be unusual to find that a marking crosses an opening on the car. There are two ways to approach this, either cut the decal before it is applied, although this will mean being absolutely sure where it lines up. Alternatively, apply the decal and, when more or less dry, carefully slice down the line using a sharp modelling knife. A small drop of setting agent will then ensure the decal follows the contours.

Final finishing

If a model has had a number of decals applied, you may find it advantageous to spray a top coat of gloss varnish. It may also

Colour schemes seem to be becoming more and more startling. This Hasegawa kit of a Porsche 944 features probably the most complex set of decals ever supplied with a kit "off the shelf". The markings are built up from over 90 separate pieces in four separate layers.

be useful over other finishes, such as metallics. Again it is vital that the previous applications—paint or decals—are absolutely dry and it could well be advisable to wash the body again, especially in the case of decal application, to remove any excess glue.

Applying a gloss varnish is exactly the same as other paint finishes, and it should be put on as 'wet' a finish as possible. However, because the varnish is not very visible it is easy to produce runs, especially to the inexperienced and, as with any finishes, a number of light coats are going to produce less problems. Some varnishes can also have an odd effect on silver—or any metallic—paint, so if there is a quantity of the latter, say window surrounds and side trim, the gloss in a heavy coat could make the silver run, so watch out!

Finally, it is perfectly feasible to polish a model car body to produce a 'showroom' finish, but care is needed. Model paints are softer than their 'full-size' equivalents and it is very easy to polish straight through the top coat! This applies particularly to transparent finishes—Candies and the like—where the finish is dependent on the layers of the paint. Polishing one area only will lighten it compared to the remainder of the body-work. As usual, "care" is the watchword and, if in doubt, practice beforehand on an old car body.

Multi-piece bodies

This concerns car bodies that are supplied in more than one piece for the basic structure. As far as 1:25 scale and larger models are concerned multi-piece bodies are the exception rather than the rule, and the reissuing of older models, mainly from Revell, has highlighted this point. A large percentage of the smaller models, however particularly the 1:32 scale from Pyro (now available as Lindbergs) are all multi-piece bodies.

In general, it should be possible to assemble the main body panels to build up what is, in effect, a one-piece body. From here the painting, detailing and assembly should follow the same pattern as a conventional one-piece bodyshell kit. However, there are going to be cases where this cannot be exactly followed; the installation of the interior may, for example, be dependent on the fact that the body sides and top are separate pieces. It is impossible to give hard and fast rules in these cases but, by careful study of the plans and the parts, it is usually possible to devise a method where most of the bodywork can be assembled 'as one', and still allow the interior or chassis to fit at a later stage. Don't be afraid to cut off parts and install them later if it helps.

Classic cars

Classic cars can be loosely defined as those with separate running boards and mudguards/fenders. From a modeller's point of view, they require a slightly different approach in their construction. They can be split into two types, which differ in construction. The smaller 'day to day' cars are available from AMT, Monogram and Revell in 1:24/5 scale, and Airfix, Matchbox and Lindberg in 1:32 scale, in both stock and custom varieties. The larger, more luxury cars, which by definition doesn't really include custom versions, appear from Heller, Italeri, AMT/MPC and Monogram in the larger scales, and Matchbox in the smaller.

Both types tend to feature a multi-piece chassis. Here the side and cross rails come as separate parts and have to be assembled before anything else is attached. The most important point is to ensure that the frame is built nice and square; any twisting will make attachment to the fender assembly difficult to say the least!

The smaller 'day to day' variety of car will probably have a one-piece body for the main shell, along with separate fenders. The interior is usually in one piece as well, and in many ways they can be treated in a similar manner to their more modern counterparts. But this does, in fact, make two-tone finishes extremely easy if the body is to be painted a different colour to the fenders assembly. Larger cars often tend to have multi-piece bodies and here the same applies as to

There are probably more conversions done to car kits, than any other genre. Here a Monogram 1937 Ford is undergoing a simple conversion to a pick-up.

the modern multi-piece bodied kits. It is usually possibly to devise some method of assembling the main bodywork as one, to allow for any filling, and painting. Again, however, every example will have to be examined on its own merits for they will all differ in detail. In general, however, it is usually possible to line up the body panels on top of the bumpers and join these together, temporarily strengthening the corners with tape.

The bonnet assembly is often a structure in its own right on these cars and, along with the radiator shell, can be kept separate. There is usually some provision for them to be displayed open to reveal the engine and you sould bear this in mind during the initial stages. Engines themselves also differ from modern blocks as far more use of brass or bronze can be found, particularly for such items as inlet manifolds. If in doubt, black, dark green or red are good stand-bys for a basic engine block colour.

Interiors on the larger classic cars also benefit from special attention. They normally arrive multi-pieced and the use of wood was far more common than in modern cars. Dash panels are a safe bet in mahogany, although some, such as AMT's 1:12 scale Cord 812, have the authentic machined-turned pattern. Note that instrument dials usually had white faces with black lettering, and not the opposite as on modern cars. Small exterior detailing was far more prevalent on these types of cars, and most would have been chromed. Many car kits provide all these details as separate parts and care will be needed to fit them into their correct position. Super glue can, in fact, be used to an advantage here, especially to hold some of the smallest parts.

Extra detailing

There are some additional details that can be added to various aspects of many model cars that do not require a great effort, but enhance the overall look. One aspect that you will find in many of the larger scale kits, 1:16 and upwards, is wiring for the engine. This is particularly noticeable in Revell's 1:16 scale dragsters, where most of the engine can be seen in all its glory. However, there is no reason why this cannot be attempted with smaller scale kits.

The wiring can be sub-divided into fuel lines, instrument runs etc, but the most noticeable are the high tension leads from the distributor to the spark plugs. The plug leads can be easily made from thin electrical wiring which is pre-coloured,

Wiring an engine is one of the simplest, but most effective additions that can be made. Some kits, such as this Revell Don Garlits rear-engined dragster, supplies all the wiring in the kit.

and black, orange or red are the most obvious choices. Thin fishing line could also be used, but it will need colouring.

Some model distributors come with the plug lead positions marked, while others are moulded in two parts. It is possible to attach the leads to these moulded pins, but in this scale it is easier to use a different approach. Use a drill bit that matches the diameter of your selected plug leads, and drill two holes into one side of the distributor so that they go straight through and out the other side. Then rotate the distributor 90° and drill two more, positioning them either slightly above or below the first. Now you have a distributor with eight holes for eight plug leads—assuming it's an eight cylinder engine. The process will need modifying for a lesser or greater number, but the principle is the same.

The pattern of the leads into the distributor may not be absolutely accurate, but in this scale is unlikely to be noticeable. This method also gives one supreme advantage in that, by threading through four lengths of wire, you end up with the eight leads, which won't suddenly come detached from the distriubtor as they go straight through. If you have used the correct diameter drill bit the leads should not need cementing, although a drop of super glue always helps.

The distributor should now be firmly fixed to the engine

block and, if in doubt, strengthen it with an additional rod, drilled and glued down the centre. Once dry, attention can be turned to the other end of the plug leads. The actual position of the plugs varies from engine to engine, though on most V-8s they are positioned down next to the exhaust manifolds. In 1:16 and larger scales it is usual to represent the white insulators of the plugs themselves, though they really aren't visible in 1:24/5 scales. Instead, drill a similar diameter hole in the correct position, cut the lead to length and super glue into place. For additional detailing, the loom that keeps the leads tidy can also be cut from plastic card, drilled and the leads pushed through before finally cementing into place.

One other easy modification is to drill out solid moulded pipes. The most obvious examples of this are exhaust pipes and fuel injection stacks. Many of the American customs and racers have these latter items usually in the form of eight (assuming a V8) long pipes sticking up through the hood With either injectors or exhausts, the first thing to do is to drill a tiny pilot hole dead centre, using a pin-vice. An electric drill is not really recommended here unless it is extremely precise, as the hole really has to be dead-centre. Then the hole has to be progressively enlarged, using as many drill bits as practical. It is tempting to drill the final hole next, but this will invariably split the plastic. The idea is to progressively drill out to get the wall as thin as possible. Once completed, the exhausts can be painted with black, while the injector stack interiors look good in bright gloss red. Gloss red is often a colour applied to the interior of other methods of air scoop, such as those found on top of blowers (superchargers) and multi-carb set-ups.

Wood and plastic

Models of pick-up trucks have always been popular in all scales and real wood can be used to create the pick-up bed itself. For the upright stakes used in many 30s and 40s style pick-up trucks, thin strips of a hard wood such as obechi or spruce can be used. Balsa wood is not the best to use because of its relatively coarse grain; the other woods have a much finer grain, which are more true to scale. The wood can either be sealed with a conventional sanding-sealer, or simply stained using conventional wood stains. It is also possible to stain using ordinary modelling paints with thinners. Balsa cement, or a contact adhesive, is best for gluing the wood to itself, but if stain is to be used, do not get the cement on parts you plan to

The American surfing era and cars are very much intertwined. This model of a 1929 Ford 'Woody' was orginally issued in the 60s as an MPC complete with surf board. In the 80s AMT reissued it as a classic of its time.

stain or it will show up. It's best to stain the parts beforehand or to pin the wood together. Final attachment to the plastic is best with the ubiquitous super glue.

Large areas of wood, such as the pick-up bed itself or possibly the side of a typical American station wagon can be cut from the very thin wood used for marquetry or veneering. New products coming onto the market are extremely thin wood cuts, with a peel-off sticky backing which are obviously much easier to work with. Using these types of wood with the standard plastic kit gives an unusual effect with only a small amount of effort and can be applied to many types, not only the pick-ups and station wagons. It is ideal for use with the older luxury classic cars with the large amount of wood panelling found in the interior.

Accessories

The model car market is extremely suitable for the accessory supplier, although these have only recenty become common within the UK. In America, there are many cottage industries supplying the car builder, from complete wiring kits for fuel lines and plug leads; upholstery kits; engine parts in resin, to miniature furry dice! Some well known American names that should be available from specialist distributors in Britain are the excellent decal sheets from Fred Cady, mainly for US Stock Cars, and Bare Metal Foil, which is probably the best way to produce a 'chromed' effect when the original isn't. This is most useful for the chrome strips and panels found on some of the more outlandish American machinery.

Closer to home comes new figures suitable for 1:24/5 scale car dioramas from both Tyresmoke Products and Freeway

Design. These give such figures, in white-metal, as US cops, 50s bobby-soxer girls and leather-jacketed boys. Tyresmoke are also issuing diorama scenes for both 50s and 80s street scenes, drag strips and track racing. Another interesting tyresmoke release was seat-belt material that splits into suitable widths for several scales in various colours. These can be used by themselves or with the fittings as supplied in some Fujimi and Hasegawa kits. They have also issued several sets of etched brass licence plates in both British and American styles, particularly useful for older style British sports cars produced by Gunze Sangyo and for US-style Hot Rods.

To complete diorama scenes, Fujimi have added what many modellers have requested for years; garage buildings and tool sets. The first set provides the main structure for a single car workshop, although basically it can be extended to make the facilities as large as you wish with additional sets. Next came the tools and equipment sets with a very complete set-up from the smallest spanner and wrench to welding equipment, tool-boxes, axle stands and even a hoist that can be positioned to hold a car aloft. This set even includes the office furniture for the garage owner—chair, table, telephone intercom and even a miniature 35 mm camera.

The third set includes four mechanic figures to work on the

Most models look best in some type of setting and cars are no exception. Fujimi have aided the modeller by providing garage, tools and mechanic figures.

vehicles. Tamiya also make figure sets, but these are to 1 : 20 scale for their Formula 1 cars, and similar individual figures for their large 1 : 12 scale car kits.

Other adaptable equipment comes in a set of parts from Italeri, intended for their truck kits, but which could be adapted to smaller vehicles.

Trucks and motorbikes

This chapter, although ostenstibly dealing with all forms of wheeled transport, has concentrated on the automobile. However, truck and motorbike modellers should not feel left out as many, if not all, of the techniques described can equally be applied to them. Wiring engines, dealing with vinyl tyres, painting and decal application cover all types of vehicles.

The first truck kit, the Peterbilt Conventional, was produced by AMT in the mid-60s, and they of course used their standard car scale, 1 : 25. These were augmented by the original trucks produced by what is now AMT's parent company, ERTL, and later added to by European trucks from Italeri in 1 : 24 scale. Revell have produced several in 1 : 25 scale and AMT added a smaller scale, 1 : 43, as they had also made several car kits in this scale. Monogram make trucks in 1 : 32 scale, snap-together, but well detailed. This company also makes the largest all-plastic truck models in 1 : 16, although the largest truck kit to date is a multi-material 1 : 8 scale monster of a Volvo tractor unit from Pocher.

Trailers are made for most of the tractor units, including Monogram's 1 : 16 scale versions. A variety of specialist trailers have also appeared over the years from flatbeds, to box-vans, double trailers and car transporters. Both AMT and ERTL in the past have had a good selection of construction equipment vehicles in their catalogues, including Caterpillar bulldozers, dump trucks and cement mixers. Revell and Italeri have concentrated on fire-fighting equipment from small Unimog-based vehicles to fire-fighting pumpers, turntable ladders and cherry-pickers. Most exotic to date is the giant Simba eight-wheel drive airport fire-engine from Revell. This equipment is all basically European, although AMT in the past have made three American LaFrance fire-fighting vehicles to 1 : 25 scale, while both Aurora and Monogram have had 1 : 32 scale pumpers as kits.

The first motorcycle kits came in 1 : 25 scale from Revell, but now the concentration is on larger scales where more detail can be used. Currently Tamiya has the largest range, in two scales 1:12 and the largest kits produced, in 1:6. The smaller range features a number of racing bikes, and rider figures can also be obtained. Gunze Sangyo selected 1:12 scale for their range of High-Tech motorbikes and these match the style of their car kits, being multi-material models. Matchbox and Heller use 1:8 scale for their motorbike kits, while ESCI use 1:9 scale for their range of unusual war-time motorbike based machinery, including the Kettenkrad half-track.

10 ACCESSORIES

TIM PERRY

Nowadays, plastic kits are marvels of mould making, using state-of-the-art production methods to incorporate detail, texture and precision of fitting, unheard of only a few years ago. Modellers perhaps take these features for granted now, particularly when considering that plastic construction kits are still really toys, aimed mainly at youngsters. These kits must be designed to assemble with the minimum of tools or materials other than standard tube cement.

Due to the very high cost of preparing a mould for even a modest model kit, often running into hundreds of thusands of pounds, only very high sales of kits will ever make such products viable in financial terms; which is, after all, the business of the kit manufacturers! Bearing this in mind, the enthusiasts should be flattered that the kit manufacturers take

Close-up of a 1:72 scale Hasegawa F/A18 Hornet with various additions. The seat is a Harrier item sold for the Sea Harrier but applicable to the F/A18 Hornet. The Head Up Display, ladder, tags and tie-down chains are from the PP Aeroparts range. Verlinden produce deck sections in resin and printed card, and a range of tractor vehicles and figures, and RBF Tags. Model Technologies also produce cockpits and canopy detail sets.

A range of products in various materials: (Backrow, left to right) PP Aeroparts' RBF Tags; Verlinden Runway (both printed paper and card); Maintrack Lightning conversion set (resin); C-Scale conversion set (white metal). (Front row) New Hope Design figures; Aeroclub and Harrier ejector seats (white metal); Model Technologies cockpit detail set (etched steel); Maintrack Buccaneer droptanks (resin); PP Models Buccaneer ladder set (etched brass and white metal).

any notice at all of their requirements, as they are outnumbered greatly by the more casual purchaser.

As it is, the kits being released today are a delight to build, with parts for alternate versions, interior details all moulded with incredible accuracy, decal sheets with every possible marking; enough to keep any modeller busy – but there are limits! Some items will be omitted because they would be too small to mould successfully with injection moulded plastic, or are of a simplified shape to enable them to come out of the mould. Others might be additions to the original subject which have been made since the kit was released, or even omissions by the kit manufacturers; mistakes do happen!

The enthusiast modeller is most interested in accuracy and realism and will take great pains to achieve these qualities in his models. To this end, he will put in a great deal of work to improve, refine or replace features on his model that have been simplified or missed by the original kit manufacturer. While some modellers will be able to build their own replacement parts, over the last five years or so there has been a boom in the so-called 'cottage industries' supplying a huge range of accessory parts aimed squarely at the enthusiast modeller. It is this phenomenon that we shall look at in this chapter.

Just a glance in any of the current modelling magazines, such as *Scale Models International,* will show a considerable number of small concerns offering accessory parts and kits specifically for the enthusiast modeller. Today the range is large indeed, and growing every day! Virtually all sections of the hobby have their own ranges of parts; aircraft modellers have metal ejector seats, undercarriage parts, ground support equipment, additional stores, conversion parts and many others. Armour modellers are well catered for with detailing sets for tanks, conversion parts, replacement small arms, ammunition, crew figures, while car and ship modellers also have wide ranges of additional components to add to their models.

A list of some of the major producers in this wide field is featured at the end of this chapter, but it is not intended to be a comprehensive list, or a recommendation of quality, but to give the reader an idea of just what is available. For up-to-date information, read the main plastic modelling magazines, who all carry adverts, as well as reviews on the various products, or ask in your local model shop. Alternatively, you can contact the producers directly. If you write to them please include a stamped addressed envelope for your reply.

Major kit manufacturers use an injection moulded plastic, usually polystyrene. It is capable of reproducing a wide range of shapes, detail and textures, very accurately. Once packaged it is robust enough to stand the rigours of life in the warehouse, shop and even in the post! Once in the hands of the modeller, it can be cut, glued, filled and painted with relative ease, and provided the kit's instructions are followed, an attractive replica will result. However, it has several features which limit the usefulness to the enthusiast; it is not very strong in thin sections, it cannot be moulded into shapes with undercuts and, most of all, it is very expensive to set up machinery to produce components using polystyrene.

Where the 'cottage industries' have made their mark is by using other processes and materials which are just as capable of similar, or better, reproduction of detail, but with much lower costs of production. While a great many different materials can be used, three have come to the fore in this hobby and these are photo-etched metal, cast plastic resins and cast white metal. All are in widespread use by the cottage industries and likely to be of interest to all modellers, whatever their particular branch of the hobby.

Fujimi BAe Hawk
with Harrier seats,
a PP Aeroparts'
tow bar, posed on
a Verlinden
printed taxiway
section. Scale is
1:72.

Photo-etching methods of production and handling

As the name suggests, this is a two-stage process. Firstly, a drawing of the component required is made very much larger than the final size, perhaps five or 10 times in many cases. The image is then reduced to the final dimensions using a graphics camera, and copied many times to fill a standard sized, 'photo-tool', which is a sandwich of two acetate photographs. Then a sheet of sensitized metal is placed between these acetate sheets and illuminated with ultraviolet light. The metal is covered with an emulsion which, after exposure, can be developed like a photograph, but instead of forming a picture, the emulsion either hardens or washes off transferring the image onto the metal surface. Next, the sheet is placed in a tank where an acid solution is sprayed at it, dissolving the exposed material while the rest is protected by the emulsion. Eventually the metal is cut right through, leaving an exact copy of the drawing, but reproduced in metal.

Some companies etch the metal from both sides at once, and the parts formed are held into a surrounding frame by small tags which have to be cut through to free the part. Other companies use a single-sided process, where the metal is supported by a plastic backing sheet. These have no tags, but the designer is limited to simple silhouettes, while the double-sided etching process allows 'half-etching', where detail, fold creases and other features can be incised into either side of the metal. More of this later!

Most types of metal can be photo-etched, but the modeller will most likely come across four; stainless steel, brass, nickel-silver and copper. Stainless steel is used mostly by US and Japanese accessory manufacturers, and gives very fine detail

Modified Hasegawa MiG 23 Flogger with PP Aeroparts' ladder and chocks. Included in these kits are numerous aerials, probes and mirrors suitable for many Soviet models. Both of these sets were designed by top Hungarian modeller, Gabor Szekeres.

when used in very thin sections. Good examples of these are Model Technologies' vast range of aircraft, ship and car parts, from cockpit sill seals to rear-view mirrors, buckles to ships railings. Being very stiff, these items are easy to handle and less likely to get bent by tweezers, but they are equally very difficult to cut from their surrounding frame! Using a good pair of scissors is the best method, cutting as closely to the part as possible. *Do not* use a scalpel; stainless is hard enough to shatter the edge, which could damage the part, or worse, cause you to slip and cut yourself. Be warned, any tags left are very hard to file away as the metal is so tough! Also, bending to shape can be awkward, as stainless doesn't much like folding. So it is best to use flat-jawed pliers right up to the line of the fold, and a very firm surface, glass, perspex/plexiglass, even a ceramic tile, and firm pressure.

Brass and copper are much easier to work with. Cutting out can be achieved with a scalpel blade and any scars can be easily cleaned up with a file, provided the part is supported well, using pliers or tweezers. Bending too can be easier, especially with curved formations where the metal will stay where it is put, while stainless will tend to spring back! But, because of their relative softness, they do demand more careful handling; gripping too hard with tweezers might mark the surface, or even buckle the thin metal. Be careful!

By using etchings attached to plastic backing sheets you will not have any scars to clean up, but you will have the problem of getting the part off the backing material! The best method is to soak the part away with a solvent and the kit instructions will suggest the appropriate one to use. Using a small brush, the part can be teased from the adhesive a bit at a time. Do not be tempted to try to flex the backing plastic as you will bend the etching as well! Once it is free, use the brush to transfer the part to some fine tissue paper to remove the solvent. Once it is dry, the part can be handled with tweezers as usual. Be extra careful with such etchings as, apart from being very small, the brass used is relatively soft and will mark or distort easily.

Nickel-silver is in between the two extremes of stiffness and ductility, but is not used much at present in the static model markets, although it may become more widespread in the future. The railway enthusiast uses it widely, especially for working valve gear on locomotives where its good strength characteristics are useful. Where stainless scores highly is its very good mirror finish, ideal for simulating chrome plate. Copper and brass can tarnish but this gives a better key for painted finishes, although it is best to use an etching primer paint before any finishing colour is applied. Car accessory shops sell small tins of zinc-based primers and these are ideal. Remember, however, to wash your brushes out with the correct thinner!

Once removed from the frame or backing sheet, the component often requires shaping, either by bending or folding. Sometimes half-etched grooves are incorporated as an aid to folding and these act like a score line on paper. Provided the component is supported up to the groove, such folds are easy to make. With larger items, trap one side of the part onto your work surface with a steel rule, right up to the groove. Then slide a scalpel blade under the protruding section and just lift slightly to start the fold. Another rule, or piece of plastic sheet can then be used to lift the part to the required angle. This technique can be used on many different structures, boxes, ladders, brackets, but all have one thing in common; you must support the metal up to the crease! This done, the assembly should go together exactly as the designer intended.

Where designs are too small to allow etched grooves, the draughtsman will sometimes incorporate small notches in the edge of the etching. Here the part should be gripped across so that the notches are just visible, using flat-jawed pliers. Gripping firmly, the protruding metal can be bent over using the flat of a scalpel blade, or the steel rule. This type of fold is often used on armour models for stowage brackets. On other designs, the folds are indicated by very thin slots between the areas to be folded, and these should be treated just like the half-etched grooves. Be very careful if the strip to be folded is narrow, as the metal will not be so weakened by this method as a half-etched groove, and so will be less easy to fold neatly.

Brass, copper and nickel-silver are all easy to solder, either to each other or to white metal, provided in this case a low-melt solder is used. However, most accessory parts will need fixing to plastic models and for this the new 'super glues', in the cyanoacrylate family, are ideal. There is a wide variety of makes available world-wide, but they come in several grades, very thin and fast-setting through to slower-setting and more viscous consistencies. Each modeller will no doubt have his favourite brands, but the slower-setting grades are useful if any adjustment in positioning is required. Hold the component in tweezers, dip carefully into a drop of glue and then apply to your model.

Whatever you do, do not apply the glue directly from the tube as you will flood the model! It is useful to test-apply the part, dry, to see just how to hold the part in the right position. Even the slower glues allow only seconds for movement, while the thinner glues can set quite literally on contact. You have been warned! Be careful with your fingers too, and heed the warnings and instructions on the glue pack. They are there for your benefit!

An alternative adhesive, particularly useful for very tiny parts, is gloss varnish. Applied with a small brush and allowed to dry slightly, parts such as gun sight rings and buckles can be eased into place with the bristles of the brush. Be patient, and keep an eye on the assembly as it will take some time to dry properly. The weight of the component may pull it out of line before the varnish has taken a grip! Once in place, additional coats of varnish or paint will secure the part, but be careful not to block up any fine detail with the paint.

Photo-etching is a tremendous technique for reproducing very fine details, and the modeller will see the already wide range of parts available expand greatly. The techniques of using etched parts are not difficult to learn, only requiring patience and care, and a steady hand; which is after all, what model-making is all about!

Cast white metal and its uses for the scale modeller

Photo-etching has one major limitation: it produces components in essentially only two dimensions. While it can be

Close-up views of PP Aeroparts' RAF oxygen trolley and Houchin Ground Power Unit. Both are kits with white metal and photo-etched parts, with decals and instructions.

surface-etched, and folded into more complex forms, it cannot produce solid 3-D items, so here another technique must be used. Casting, where a liquid is poured into a cavity where it then hardens into a solid shape, is a basic method dating from the Bronze Age. Nowadays, we have more advanced materials but the principle remains. Two casting processes will be looked at, using metal and resin; firstly the metal.

The moulds for casting white metal are usually made from a rubber compound, either vulcanised with heat and pressure, or from a silicone rubber, which is cured with a chemical catalyst. With the vulcanising process, metal patterns are placed between two discs of raw rubber, the whole assembly is then placed in a metal container and pressed with a hydraulic ram. Up to 30 tons pressure is applied, and the sandwich is heated for a controlled time and temperature. This causes a chemical change in the rubber, setting it to the shape of the patterns and toughening it to just the same consistency of a car tyre.

Once separated, the patterns are removed and channels cut into the rubber leading to a central chamber. Metal studs are usually placed surrounding the mould which act as locators.

When used, the mould is placed between two pressure plates inside a cabinet, and spun to a controlled speed. Molten white metal is then poured into the centre of the mould and centrifugal force throws the metal outwards into the cavities. After a set time the spinning mould is stopped, the cabinet lid opened and the mould split to release the solidified metal. Then the rubber mould comes into its own; being flexible, any undercuts on the pattern can be released by simply bending the mould! There are of course limits, but very intricate shapes are possible which would be impossible to extract from a hard injection mould.

Silicone moulds are made in a different manner. The raw material is liquid and it is mixed with a hardener, then poured into a mould containing the patterns. These can be of virtually any materials, as no heat or pressure is involved; plastic, metal, card, even fabric can all be used! The mould halves are poured one at a time, allowing time to cure between. The main disadvantages are the expense (the silicone rubber is not cheap), the curing time (several days instead of several hours), and the final mould is not as strong as a vulcanised item. However, against that, the vulcanising process requires metal patterns and, for the small producer, preparing these may not be possible.

White metal components can be treated in very similar ways to plastic parts, as the metal is relatively soft and can be cut, filed and glued, with cyanoacrylates or epoxies, using the same tools. Files will clog if used heavily, but can be cleaned out with wire-card, available from a tool shop. Depending on the grade of metal, the parts may be easy to bend or quite brittle, so be very careful if trying to straighten a part.

Sometimes the metal will oxidise slightly, giving a dull grey surface rather than bright metal. This is easily removed with a file, emery paper or even a glass-fibre brush, available from drawing office suppliers as an eraser. However, be careful of the fibres as they can irritate the skin very badly! Once assembled, the same primer used on the etchings can be used to give a good base for the top coat.

Assembly of white metal parts can be a little more challenging than a plastic kit, as often a deal more 'fitting' is required. 'Flash', where metal has spread out of the part between the moulds, can be easily removed with blade and file but, if you find the halves of the mould are badly out of register, you are advised to return the part to the manufacturer for

A trio of resin airfield accessory kits, to 1:48 scale, from the Belgian firm of Verlinden Productions who also produce a host of other accessory items for military and aircraft modellers.

replacement! Test-fitting, and thorough reading of any instructions with your kit are a must; some accessory kits are less than well endowed with instructions, sometimes only an exploded diagram is given. You must be sure of how the assembly is made, and that it all fits before applying the glue. Modelling clay, bulldog clips, even twisted wire can often be used to jig parts in the correct place as adhesive is put into the joins. A scalpel blade or pin can be very useful for this.

So, white metal is ideal for intricate details, as well as some larger parts. It is easy to work and, with a little care, can be used alongside plastics with equal success. Two warnings though! First, in large lumps its weight can cause problems; for example, using metal for drop-tanks on aircraft, where the plastic undercarriage may not be up to supporting the extra weight. Second, most white metals contain lead, and other metals which are not very good for you if ingested. Wash your hands thoroughly after handling it, and *do not eat, drink or smoke* at your modelling table.

Cast resins for the scale modeller
In small sections, white metal is ideal as a production material. In larger amounts, however, it is heavy, expensive and susceptible to distortion during shrinkage, so another material is required. Here, modern technology has again come to our rescue with plastic resins which harden when mixed with a

catalyst. There are many families of such resins, and literally hundreds of grades of resin within each family, but the modeller is likely to come across only a few of these. Until recently the major types were polyester and epoxy resins, as used on fibre-glass and familiar to most in the form of car body repair kits, canoes and motorcycle fairings.

These resins are quite viscous and take some time to cure, ranging from several hours to several days. Not much of a problem for the individual, but as a production material not very useful. Also, great care is required to avoid overheating the material as it gives considerable heat as it cures, which causes crazing, distortion or worse! That said, there are several short run productions, all made by skilled individuals on 'a couple for me, a couple for my friends' basis which are every bit as good as conventional kits. Watch the classified ads in the magazines!

More recently, the rise of the use of polyurethane resins has revolutionised the manufacture of more solid accessories. These materials are related to the cyanoacrylate 'super glues' and cure in a few minutes. Additionally, they are very runny before curing and this allows moulds to fill easily, although most producers use some additional methods of removing air bubbles, which are the bane of resin casters!

The moulds are prepared from full-size patterns sculpted in every last surface detail, using plastic, putty, clay, brass or virtually any other material. Moulds are prepared using the same silicone rubber material that can be used for the white metal, although they tend to be much larger to allow large keys between the mould sections for accurate alignment. A release agent is sprayed into the mould halves which are then assembled and the resin/hardener mix poured into the cavity. This can be injected with a pressurised system, or just by gravity, but the mould is then placed into a vacuum chamber and the air pressure reduced. Any bubbles then expand and float out of the mould leaving a completely filled cavity. After a period of time, the resin will have cured sufficiently for the mould to be split open and the part removed ready for cleaning and packing.

Once it is in the modeller's hands, he will be impressed by the surface detail possible with this material, and the accuracy; shrinkages with these resins is measured in small fractions of a percentage point! It also lacks the tacky feel sometimes found on polyester castings. Large pouring points can be easily removed with a razor saw or scalpel, where the excellent cutting and shaping properties will become apparent. It can be shaped and drilled with ease, and cyanoacrylate glues work extremely well, so attaching to plastic or metal parts is very straightforward.

It is advisable to wash the resin castings, using warm soapy water and a soft brush to remove any release agent as this may stop paint adhering but, after this is done, enamel or acrylic paints can be used successfully; it really is a wonderful material to use!

Polyurethane resins do have a couple of drawbacks though. The first is that they can smell rather, an odour reminiscent of grannie's wardrobe (camphor mothballs) which can be a bit overpowering. This does, however, disperse with time. Second, any air trapped in the mould during casting will result in dimples in the surface and these can be filled with either epoxy putties like Milliput, or the thicker gap-filling cyano-acrylate adhesives. Because the resin is very good at reproducing fine detail, some manufacturers try to get *everything* on their models, with often less than satisfactory results. For instance, tool clips on tank hulls are better removed and replaced with either plastic strip or, if available, etched parts. Sometimes manufacturers design kits from different materials to complement each other, the Top Brass and MAC kits being good examples of this.

Examples of etched, cast metal and cast resin accessories in action!

It would be impossible to list all of the products in these classes that are available world-wide. However, to illustrate just some of the possibilities, I will give two modelling examples, taking a basic plastic kit and a number of accessory kits currently available in the UK. Some of these items may be difficult to obtain locally if you live outside the UK, but the major mail

Matchbox's Buccaneer kit ejector seat compared with Harrier's white metal version at right.

order houses will be delighted to assist you! The first example, the HS Buccaneer S2B, is a relatively simple kit produced by Matchbox and aimed squarely at the younger modeller. It comes with over-emphasised panel lines, multi-coloured plastic and some details like the cockpit, undercarriage and underwing stores simplified or missing. The model has been left unpainted to illustrate the numerous parts used. Please refer to Chapter 7 for finishing techniques.

The cockpit is often the focal point of an aircraft model, especially the seat. Here white metal seats made by Harrier, a divison of Chota Sahib, can be used to good advantage. The close-up photo (on page 199) comparing the plastic seat and its metal counterpart shows instantly the improvement! The seat firing handles are from the PP Aeroparts range, accessories for accessories!

The modeller will still have to use his skills to rebuild the cockpits for this model, as even the instrument coamings and rear cockpit clear blast screen are missing from the original kit design. The canopy can also be replaced, and Canovak produce exactly the right part in their range of moulded acetate canopies. Also extensive cleaning-up of the airframe will be needed, and the jet pipes opened up. The intakes can be used from the kit, or if a model of the earlier Royal Navy S1 version is required, Maintrack Models come to the rescue with a conversion set of three castings in a very fine polyester resin. These are the smaller intakes of this version, and the plain bomb-bay door without the RAF fuel tank, as fitted to the Matchbox kit. However, the example given here has the S2B intakes.

The Matchbox kit comes completely devoid of underwing stores, and so one of the C-Scale accessory kits has been used, providing weapons pylons, laser-guided bombs, additional aerials, intakes, blisters and ECM pods, as well as IFR probe and missile rail. These can all be used in various combinations, with details and other references given in the illustrated instructions. Parts are also given for the 'Slipper Tanks' but the modeller may feel the weight of these might be too much for his model, and so resin castings from the Maintrack Models range can be substituted. Either way, some fitting, filling and filing will be needed to achieve a good finish.

This leaves the airframe looking more like the real thing, but most aircraft modellers like to display their models on some sort of base, a runway or hardstanding for instance. These can

The much modified and improved Matchbox Buccaneer kit (see text).

be made of pre-printed card items, such as those in the Verlinden Productions range but when parked there is a lot of ground equipment to be found round modern aircraft! For modellers of modern jets, the PP Aeroparts range has many useful kits, and on this model, the Buccaneer ladder set, wheel chocks, tow bar have been used and on the base a Houchin Ground Power Unit and fire extinguishers. Also printed paper 'Remove Before Flight' tags, as well as the seat firing handles mentioned above.

For modellers of WW2 RAF aircraft a range of bomb handling trolleys, tractors and other vehicles is available from Lead Sled Models. Notice the Aeroparts ladder set also contains windscreen wipers, aileron push rods and fuel dump end plates for this aircraft. Crew figures can also be purchased, cast in white metal. Two pilots from the Airwaves series are shown, although Verlinden have added some resin US Navy deck figures to their extensive range, which includes some aircraft items, but more armour parts.

To show a more major usage of accessories, especially polyurethane resin, we now move to the armour modelling branch of the hobby. The basic plastic kit used here is made by Tamiya, one of the most prestigious kit manufacturers. The subject is the M4 Sherman tank, the most widely used Allied tank of WW2, used in many versions in nearly all theatres of

Some of the white metal figures available to aircraft modellers: (Left to right)

RAF and USAF crew (painted) from Airwaves; pilot figures, 1:48 and 1:72 scales from New Hope Design, with a 1:32 Israeli Kfir pilot standing behind.

The Tamiya M4 converted with MAC and Top Brass kits seen before painting.

Top Brass Sherman detail set, with over 200 individual parts! Etched metal is ideal for such parts, reproducing exactly items such as light guards, tool clips etc.

operations. There is tremendous scope for conversions on this basic model.

This is reflected in the large number of conversion and accessory kits for this model and we have chosen MAC kits of replacement hull and turret parts, in polyurethane and white metal, Top Brass detailing sets for the Sherman and 50 calibre Browning machine gun. Crew figures, cast in white metal are from the Top Brass range as well, while ammunition boxes, blanket rolls, spare wheels and periscopes are from Verlinden. Photo-etched barbed wire comes from Pro-Mods while the replacement tracks are again Top Brass parts.

It can be easily seen from the comparative photos how much more detail can be incorporated into a model by using these accessory kits. Many items have been replaced completely, for example the light guards and tool brackets, the plastic items being grossly over-scale. Some parts were not even attempted by the kit moulder, such as the periscope guards. The resin hull and turret components have allowed a completely different version to be modelled, and with other similar combinations a range of models could be made portraying the entire history of development of the vehicle.

Other detail parts, such as the stores, spare parts and wire, allow a 'personalised' model to be created, different from all others, and yet retaining the scale authenticity needed by the modeller. The etched metal, in particular, lends itself to bending to simulate battle damage exactly, and latches look as if they would really work! Two rather special items, the Browning MG and the tracks, offer the ultimate in detail, the gun having over 20 parts where the plastic item in the original kit has only four! The tracks are formed from injection moulded

Close-up of alternate tracks from the Top Brass range, for the M4 Sherman. Individual links are moulded in polystyrene, with cast metal end connectors. While a bit tedious to assemble, they are very realistic.

plastic links, (one case where the economics of quantity, as well as a relatively simple mould made economic sense!) with cast metal end connectors. While time-consuming to apply, the end result is far more realistic than the polythene items in the original kit, and allow one of six different tread patterns to be used.

Accessories: to use or not to use

By starting with a standard kit, a little extra time and the help of some of the 'cottage industry' products, the modeller can turn a simple toy into a realistic model of his chosen subject. Accessories such as these are not a short cut to modelling success, if anything, they demand more from their users as several new techniques must be learnt before they can be successfully applied. Some modellers may shun the use of such accessories, either on the grounds of cost, or the idea that such 'bolt-on goodies' have less worth than hand-made items.

Well, you must make up your own mind on this! However,

A completed Sherman model using MAC hull conversion set and Top Brass detailing parts. The realism is self-evident! Model by Ian Phillips.

using such a wide range of different materials will expand the skills of the modeller, and certainly help speed up the modelling process. All of the accessory manufacturers are skilled modellers in their own right and this is one way of sharing their talents with us all. All have started their businesses from their own great interest in the hobby, and they deserve the enthusiasts' support!

MAJOR ACCESSORY MANUFACTURERS

ACCURATE ARMOUR LTD,
Unit 16,
Ardgowan Street Industrial Estate,
Port Glasgow PA14 5DG.
Tel: 0475-43955.

AEROCLUB MODELS,
5 Silverwood Avenue,
Ravenshead,
Nottingham NG15 9BU.
Tel: 0602-670044.

AKITA,
22 Quicks Road,
London SW19 1EZ.
Tel: 01-540 2947.

C-SCALE, from:
ED Models,
64 Stratford Road,
Shirley,
Solihull,
West Midlands B90 3LP.
Tel: 021-744 7488.

CANOVAC,
50 Elsa Road,
Welling,
Kent DA16 1JS.

FOTOCUT,
Erieville Road,
Box 120,
Erieville,
NY 13061,
USA.
UK importers:

Croyden Impex,
2 Kingsburgh Court,
East Linton,
East Lothian EH40 3BL.

GOLD MEDAL MODELS,
12332 Chapman Avenue,
No. 81 Garden Grove,
CA 92640, USA.
UK importers:
White Ensign Models,
35 Madeline Place,
Chelmsford,
Essex CM1 4XD.
Tel: 0245-441480.

HARRIER,
'Chota Sahib',
124 Springfield Road,
Brighton,
Sussex BN1 6DE.
Tel: 0273-566326.

LEAD SLED MODELS,
Unit 3,
The Round House Craft Centre,
Buckland In The Moor,
Ashburton,
Devon TQ13 7HN.
Tel: 0364-52971.

M & E MODELS,
62 Periwinkle Close,
Sittingbourne,
Kent ME10 2JU.

MAINTRACK MODELS,
79 Queens Road,
Hastings,
East Sussex TN34 1RL.
Tel: 0424-437428.

MINIATURE AUTOBITS,
Distributed by Tyresmoke
Products, see right.

MODEL TECHNOLOGIES,
15561 Product Lane,
Unit D16,
Huntingdon Beach,
CA 92649,
USA.
UK importers:
Hannants,
Trafalgar House,
29-31 Trafalgar St.,
Lowestoft,
Suffolk NR23 3AT.
Tel: 0502-565688.

PP MODELS,
Unit 12,
Station Road Workshops,
Station Road,
Kingswood,
Bristol BS15 4PR.
Tel: 0272-575577, ext 222.

PRO-MODS,
25 Bourneville Road,
Whitehall,
Bristol BS5 9AL.

SCALE LINK,
42 Appleby Close,
Twickenham,
Middlesex TW2 5NA.
Tel: 01-894 2006.

TOP BRASS,
Produced by Tyresmoke
Products, see below.

TYRESMOKE PRODUCTS,
Tyresmoke Products,
21 Brampton Court,
Bowerhill,
Melksham,
Wiltshire SN12 6TH.
Tel: 0225-706999.

VERLINDEN,
Verlinden Productions,
Berlaarsestraat 36,
2500 Lier,
Belgium.
UK importers:
Historex Agents,
3 Castle Street,
Dover,
Kent CT16 1QJ.
Tel: 0304-206720.

This list is not intended to be a comprehensive directory of 'cottage industries', but a selection of those ranges that I have personally found to be very useful. There are many other ranges available, and their omission should not be taken as a slur on the quality of their products!

As you will see, several concerns have already grown into industrial units such has been the demand for their products. Equally, a lot of names disappear as quickly as they arise, either folding for lack of business control, or absorbed into other more established ranges. The only way to keep up with the current state of ranges is to read the modelling press, such as *Scale Models International*, on a regular basis.

11   SHIP MODELLING

GRAHAM DIXEY

Among the vast range of subjects available as plastic kits, model ships probably offer the greatest scope for improvement. This is because the prototype is usually so huge (requiring a considerable degree of scaling down), and so complex externally (requiring much simplification). By contrast, most aeroplanes and cars are relatively 'clean' and the same loss of detail does not necessarily occur. It is fortunate that modern ships, especially warships, are fairly angular because it is then easier to refine existing details or add new ones from available plastic materials, such as card, strip and rod.

During its lifetime, a particular ship, because of modifications, may alter its appearance quite markedly, allowing the modeller opportunities to produce a model, (or even several) of a given ship at a time in her life other than that represented by the kit maker. Further, ships tend to be built in classes, with recognisable differences between the various named vessels of that class. This also provides scope for the modeller in that one particular kit can be used as the basis for any of the ships in that class.

Availability of kits
Today's modellers are fortunate in the vast range of kits available, largely due to the enterprise of the Japanese makers, whose output is quite prolific. However, there are also some European manufacturers with excellent ranges of kits so that, between east and west, the market contains more than enough to keep the avid ship modeller busy for as many years as his enthusiasm and faculties survive!

The following review will give some idea of what is available. It will quickly be noted that the modeller of WW2 warships comes off best, while the lover of merchant ships has a much more limited choice. For the period modeller in plastic, there is

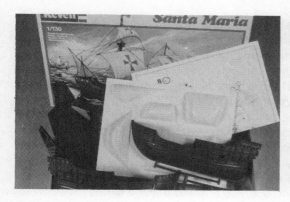

The type of sailing ship kit that the beginner ought to tackle. Still an interesting choice of prototype but without the rigging complications of a larger vessel. On such a model you can learn a little about the basic principles of rigging.

also a sizeable selection of kits around. One perennial problem for the scale modeller is evident here as in other fields: that is the matter of scale. There is no standard scale.

There are one or two popular scales, of which 1:700 is an example, notably for waterline models and 1:350 for larger, more detailed full-hull models. These are supplemented by a profusion of scales, some of which have obviously been chosen for no other reason than that they produced suitable-sized kits for the manufacturer! Taking the makers in alphabetical order, then:

Airfix The range of this maker, after some thin years, is now improving with some notable reissues. At 1:600 scale there are now eight kits, all WW2. British – the carriers *Victorious* and *Ark Royal*, battleships *Hood* and *Nelson*, cruiser *Belfast*; German – *Bismarck, Graf Spee* and *Scharnhorst*. There is also a RAF Rescue Launch at 1:72 scale. A range of classic ships includes, at various scales, such great names as *Cutty Sark, Victory, Wasa, Bounty,* etc. There is also a kit for the P.S. *Great Western*, Brunel's classic sail/paddler.

Aoshima This maker produces a range of 29 1:700 waterline models, all apparently WW2, 21 of which are of Japanese prototypes. There are three passenger boats in the range. Other vessels included are *Bismarck* and *Tirpitz, North Carolina* and *Washington, Illustrious* and *Victorious.*

Doyusha There are just two ship models from this maker, both being motorised submarines, the Japanese I-401 and the German Type VIIC.

Fujimi This is another Japanese maker who has produced a range of 1:700 scale waterline models. There are six aircraft carriers, nine battleships, eight cruisers, four destroyers, two submarines and three packs of carrier planes to the same scale for IJN, RN and USN carriers. Nineteen of the above kits are of Japanese prototypes but, interestingly, the choice of foreign ships includes the *Lexington, Saratoga, Ark Royal* and *Eagle* among the carriers and the *New Jersey* and *Deutschland* among the battleships.

Hasegawa This maker has two ranges, the 1:450 scale Famous Warship Series and a 1:700 scale waterline series. The former runs to eight models, as follows—*Yamato, Missouri, Musashi, Vanguard, Bismarck, Shinano, Tirpitz* and *Akagi*. The waterline series includes four carriers (among them the US carriers *Essex* and *Hancock*), four battleships (including the US ships *Alabama* and *South Dakota*), ten cruisers, eight destroyers, a liner (and the hospital ship version of it) and three submarine kits.

With the exception of one of the submarine kits (types VIIC and IXC), all of the latter are of Japanese prototypes. There is also a harbour set, a tugger set and sets of IJN and USN aeroplanes, all to 1:700 scale.

Helier-Humbrol This maker produces kits to the scales of 1:200 and 1:400. At the former scale there are three models, the *Marie Jeanne*, the *Roc Amadour* and the *Smitt Rotterdam/London* and eight period ships that include *La Sirene*, the *Mayflower* and the *Golden Hind*. The 1:400 scale range comprises seven warships and includes, as one might expect, some French vessels, notably the *Clemenceau* and the *Foch*.

Imai Another Japanese maker but with a rather different range, including some very large and very expensive kits, e.g. the *Nippon Maru* at £99.99 at the time of writing! Within the range can be found Roman and Greek warships, a chebec and galleas, a junk, the *Cutty Sark*, USS *Susquehanna* and so on. A very wide time scale indeed.

Italeri The small selection of kits available from this maker are at either 1:700 or 1:720 scale (virtually compatible with 1:700 scale). These include modern US and Russian submarines (there is also a kit of the USSR *Typhoon* at 1:350 scale), the

Hood, Graf Spee, Deutschland, Lützow, Admiral Scheer, plus four US nuclear carriers—*Roosevelt, Nimitz, Eisenhower* and *Carl Vinson.*

Matchbox This range includes 1:700 waterline models of WW2 ships including HMS *Exeter,* HMS *Ariadne,* USS *Fletcher,* to name just three recent re-issues. Not seen before from other makers are the USS *San Diego,* USS *Indianapolis* and HMS *Duke of York.* There is also a kit for a Flower Class corvette at 1:72 scale, that will also be available as an R/C conversion.

Monogram The maker's catalogue lays claim to two series, the Navy Ship Assortment and the Tall Ship Assortment, all moulded to a length of 16 inches or more, and a very large model (33 ½ in. long) of the carrier USS *Enterprise.* The above assortments contain respectively the *Kitty Hawk, New Jersey* and *Tirpitz,* and the *Cutty Sark,* USS *Constitution* and USS *United States.* However, this maker has also issued some interesting 'pairings' in a new series of 'Air/Sea Combat sets', in which a 16 in. model of the USS *Nimitz* is kitted together with a 1:72 scale F-4 Phantom II and a similar kit is made up of the USS *Kitty Hawk* with an F-14 Tomcat.

Nichimo As well as a 30 cm motorised series (27 models—WW2 and modern), this maker has a range of 17 warships (except one ice-breaker) at a variety of scales; 1:200, 1:300, 1:500 and 1:700. The largest of these is a 1:200 scale kit for the Japanese battleship, *Yamato,* which retails at £137.50!

Revell The Revell range is wide in scope and even wider in the choice of scales. These latter have been chosen to provide a

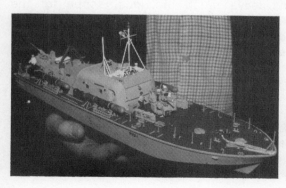

Tamiya's 'Vosper Perkasa Fast Patrol Boat', a highly detailed kit, modelled here by Peter Schofield.

Some makers give
the easy choice of
a waterline or full-
hull model.

'sensible' size of model whatever the subject. Thus the little *Santa Maria,* kitted at a scale of 1 : 130 makes up to a model of 21.4 cm l.o.a., while the very much larger *Cutty Sark* is found in the scales of 1 : 350 (24.1 cm l.o.a.) and 1 : 220 (40 cm l.o.a.). Kits from this maker cover a wide range of sailing ships, ocean liners (e.g. RMS *Titanic*), modern specialised ships (e.g. RV *Meteor*) as well as WW2 and later, including some submarines with detailed interiors.

Tamiya This maker has two main ranges, in scales of 1 : 350 and 1 : 700, as well as two modern patrol boats in 1 : 72 scale. The former range includes *Tirpitz, Bismarck, Yamato, Musashi, King George V, Prince of Wales, Enterprise, Missouri* and *New Jersey.* The 1 : 700 waterline series runs to 34 kits, all WW2 and mostly Japanese. Ships of interest in the range include the *Rodney* and the carrier *Hornet.* There is also a harbour accessory set as well as a tugger set.

While the general standard of all of the above is very good, natural limitations leave much individual scope for the modeller to impress his own personality upon the end result. There is also much that can be done in the way of displaying the finished model. This should be given as much thought as the modelling itself. After all, it isn't doing the model justice if it is not shown to its best advantage. It is this aspect that will be considered next.

Displaying ship models
First of all, there are two possible presentations—waterline or full-hull. The choice is an individual matter. A full-hull model shows the underwater lines, the propulsion, bilge keels, etc, so

is more 'technically' interesting. A waterline model shows the ship as she appears in her natural element, the sea. Some representation of the sea, no matter how simple, must really be provided to do justice to this method. It is quite easy to get this desired effect, as will be shown.

A full-hull model is usually expected to be seen supported on some form of stand, as in a museum. Kits generally include a stand which has to be constructed from several plastic components. This is usually the first part to be discarded, as far as I am concerned! A pair of polished brass rods, fitted into a varnished mahogany stand and inserted into holes drilled in the keel, make for a much better appearance. Polished acrylic rods are also an excellent bet; in fact the entire base could, with advantage, be made from acrylic sheet and rod, giving the effect of the model being just suspended above the table top. What is not wanted is the appearance of it sitting in a heavy cradle.

A totally different approach to displaying a full-hull model is to set it in a suitable cut-out in a piece of acrylic sheet. This represents the surface of the sea and is set several inches above a representation of the sea bed, within a box that is glazed on all sides. Thus, it becomes possible to look at the ship from unusual angles, including upwards from the sea bed. The principal difficulty with this method lies in determining the exact shape of cut-out for the hull, and in making the sea bed look realistic. The latter will have to include items such as rocks, beds of seaweed, even part of a wreck, etc, otherwise there is nothing to hold the viewer's attention.

My preference is for waterline models as these show the ship in her natural environment. If the kit is for a waterline model (our kit round-up showed that many kits fell into this class),

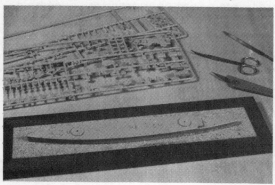

It is usually easier to work on a waterline model if the basic hull and main-deck assembly is stuck down on the base. White PVA glue is suitable.

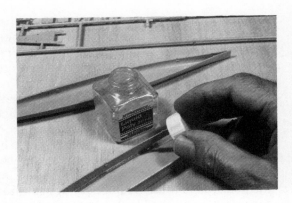

If the waterline option is chosen, a strengthening plate has to be fitted at the waterline. in the larger models some plastic card bulkheads should be fitted as well.

then it is simply a matter of attaching the model to a suitable base and applying a 'modelled' sea around it. The term 'modelled' is used very loosely here. If the kit is for a full-hull model, then part of the hull has to be removed to convert it into a waterline model. The upper hull must be suitably strengthened when this has been done.

Some enterprising manufacturers now recognise the need for some choice in the matter and mould a hull which can be easily parted to become a waterline model or be reassembled as a full-hull model. Without this facility, it is necessary to determine the waterline, mark it around the hull boldly and saw through it carefully with a razor saw. The cut edge of the upper hull should then be rubbed firmly on a medium grade abrasive paper to eliminate the saw marks.

The sea can be 'modelled' in one of three principal ways:

(a)   The first is the easiest. The base around the model, for the full area of the sea, is painted in shades of deep blue, blue-green, brownish-green, etc, as seems appropriate, or combinations of these, as the sea is rarely constant in colour. Either enamel or acrylic paint is equally suitable for this. When this is dry, a number of coats of gloss varnish are applied over it, until the appearance seems about right. This is for a flat calm.

To put some motion into it, PVA glue can be laid quite thickly over the surface, prior to varnishing, in a series of waves; a brush will help to spread it out into the required pattern. This dries more or less clear. Several coats can be given if required. When the surface has enough variation in it, the tops of the 'waves' should be given flicks of white paint to produce the 'sea horses' that characterise water in motion. When all is dry, the

(Left). The sea modelled in plaster, painted in acrylics and varnished to support Italeri's Frogmen set. A model by the author. (Below) A Vosper M.T.B. modelled by Dave Beavis. The bow wave, in painted plaster, is especially effective.

coats of varnish can be applied as before. This method is suitable for the smaller scales such as 1:700.

(b)   For larger scales, or simply very rough seas where waves of real height are required, plaster is ideal for sculpting the wave formation. In this case, the ship's hull should be packed up on the base at the desired angle and height, and fairly wet plaster trowelled under and around the hull. Once all the plaster is in place, the actual wave formation can be coaxed into shape by using a large, wet paintbrush; a decorator's half-inch or one-inch brush is often suitable. It is quite easy to get very realistic waves this way, stroking the wet plaster firmly with the brush and ending some strokes with a little flick up and around to create wind-swept waves.

When the plaster is dry it should be primed and painted, well-thinned deep blue/blue-green into the hollows, pale blue-green to pure white at the crests. A coat or two of satin varnish over all, when dry, completes the effect. A non-shrinking plaster is best, such as Tetrion, but only in thin layers. Several light applications are better than one heavy one.

(c)   A third method uses the clear casting resin that can be obtained in craft or model shops. The base must have a lip all round to contain the depth of resin to be used. The sea bed must be painted first. The method is not intended to be a substitute for that described earlier using acrylic sheet for the sea. It is impracticable to use what is a very expensive medium for anything other than quite nominal depths.

The only advantage of this method is that, if the layers of resin are graduated in intensity from the surface downwards, there is perhaps a greater sense of realism than with other methods. The sea-bed should not be seen in detail however. The method will normally be applied to full-hull models, of course, and small ones at that, since the amount of resin needed is excessive. The successive layers should not exceed 5 mm depth at the most. Dyes can be added to the resin to provide the graduation mentioned earlier.

Improving and super-detailing

To improve the realism of a ship model, two areas should be considered. These are, the reduction in size of over-scale parts, and the addition of parts that have been omitted because of limitations in the moulding process. Scale very largely dictates how far the modeller can go in these endeavours. The rule is, 'if in doubt, leave it out'!

The superstructure of a warship or liner often reveals

This is a useful accessory if detailed assemblies are to be built up, piece by piece. The actual assembly can be held in the tips of fine tweezers.

An obvious improvement to realism, easy to carry out, is the drilling out of the scuttles.

excessive thickness of the screens, for example. Surfaces that should be vertical often slope at 1–2 degrees, the draught angle needed for the moulding process. Improvements can be effected by either scraping down or cutting out parts of the structure and replacing it with substitutes, more nearly to scale, made from plastic card. What is attempted depends largely upon the modeller's skill and having to hand drawings/ photos of the real thing.

Parts that should be hollow may be moulded solid. Such details include gun barrels of main armament, scuttles, funnel vents, hawse-holes, etc. Except for gun barrels, in most scales it is an easy matter to drill these out with fine drill bits held in a pin-vice. Polystyrene is a very tractable material in this respect. The bridge glazing may be represented by engraved lines. This

(Top left) The circular mould marks, clearly seen in this view, will ruin the appearance of the deck unless something is done about them. (Above) The first step is to scrape them out using the edge of a sharp knife blade . . . (Left) . . . and then re-engrave the deck planking with the tip of a fine file held against a straight edge.

Some of the more complex areas can, with advantage, be treated as separate sub-assemblies and constructed as such, including their painting.

can also be drilled out and filed to shape with needle files. Only in the larger scales is actual glazing feasible.

Joints in assemblies must be made invisible by ensuring the surfaces are properly in contact while the cement is setting and by scraping and rubbing down well after assembly. The weather decks must show no sign of a gap when cemented into the hull. Strips of sellotape should be used to hold the assembly firmly while liquid cement is run into the joint and while it is setting, allowing overnight for this.

All parts should be examined carefully to see where moulded-in detail can be scraped off and built up more realistically. This applies to such items as steam pipes on funnels (replace with plastic rod), watertight doors, hatches, winches, breakwaters, etc. It is possible to scrape down the entire weather deck, planking and all, and re-engrave it, building up the detail with plastic card, rod and heat-stretched sprue. It is vital to keep a record of the deck layout once the detail has been removed. Ideally, drawings and/or photographs of the vessel being modelled are desirable.

Among the areas that should be scrutinised are the armament. If the secondary armament is over-scale, it is quite easy to use scraps of plastic card and heat-stretched sprue to build it anew. Blast covers can be added to the main armament

Painting and construction can proceed hand in hand. This photo shows that later, smaller details have been added after a large part of the structure has been painted.

by moulding some Milliput (epoxy putty) around the gun barrels at the turret openings.

The ships' boats and launching gear should also be looked at. Again heat-stretched sprue can be useful for making up new davits. If the ships' boats are much over-scale, it is probably best to scrap them and make new ones from Milliput. Any modeller who hasn't tried this versatile medium is advised to do so. It is possible to make extremely fine details with it; there is plenty of working time and it dries rock hard, in which state it can be cut, sawn, filed, etc., and will take paint without priming. It can be used just like Plasticine, for those modellers whose sculptural development hasn't advanced beyond this stage, and can be formed with the tip of a craft knife, toothpick, cocktail stick, etc.

Lattice masts and aerials can be made from heat-stretched sprue. It is possible to draw this out into such fine filaments that it can be used for aerial wires, stays, etc. Masts and booms on small-scale models can also be made from this material.

This brings us to the question of how to deal with the masts, yards and rigging of sailing ships. In general, these kits tend to be of a generous size, which means the rigging can't be ignored. On very small sailing ship models, the impracticability of rigging them accurately justifies leaving out most of the details. Kit makers rarely give anything other than the sketchiest of details of the rigging and the only way to rig a sailing ship model properly is to learn what every rope, block and sheave, etc., does in the full size. Armed with this understanding, the modeller can tackle the subject constructively. At the end of this chapter you will find some references that can be very useful if they can be tracked down or borrowed from a library.

The best source of detail is the real thing. This view up *Discovery's* foremast is quite revealing. Note the iron-work to support the yard, the shroud details, the construction of the cross-trees, etc.

Note the various ways of belaying ropes. Pins are seen on the pin-rails and around the mast-band; some ropes are belayed to iron rings in the deck.

The rigging of a sailing ship falls into two groups—standing rigging and running rigging. The former consists of all of the stays and shrouds, etc, that brace the masts and take the strains of sailing. The running rigging is variable and is used to work the ship, that is to raise and lower and trim the sails, to set the vessel on a given tack, etc. The subject is fascinating to study and worth doing so if models of this type are contemplated. In order to produce a satisfying model it is also essential to know something of the construction of the masts and spars, how the latter are fitted to the masts and so on. Such details are rarely shown in plastic kits.

Moulded-on 'wooldings' (rope whippings) on the masts can be scraped off and replaced with something like the real thing by using thread. Shrouds, as provided by most kit makers, are

A sharp knife (or sharp, pointed scissors) easily detaches etched metal parts from the sheet. Handling calls for tweezers.

always unbelievably awful—the ratlines (the horizontal foot-ropes tied at intervals) should normally be much finer than the shrouds themselves. There is no easy way to make them. It can be done on the model or on a nail jig, the main ingredient being patience.

Now for the thorny subject of sails. A static model on a stand looks far better without any at all. Whether set or furled they invariably look unrealistic. They are usually represented in kits these days with vacform mouldings, better than they used to be but still not much good. If sails are essential they can be made by soaking tissue in weak tea and pressing it carefully over a former; easily made by moulding some plasticine in the hands. When dry they should be sprayed with varnish. The seam lines between adjacent vertical strips of cloth can be lightly pencilled on.

Etched metal accessories

A development that now helps the modeller to get a finer scale appearance without too much sweat is the etched-metal sheet. Where they are available for the model under construction, they offer the chance to have really finely-made radars, lattice masts, railings and ladders, aircraft propellers, cranes, searchlight masts, depth charge tracks, safety nets and many other such details.

The major maker of these is Loren Perry (Gold Medal Models) and they are available in the UK from White Ensign Models of 35 Madeline Place, Chelmsford, Essex. They are mostly 1:700 or 1:350 scale, for a limited range of ships, mostly IJN at present but expanding; there is an excellent range of 1:700/1:350 scale decals available to complement these sets. The same maker has also published a useful book,

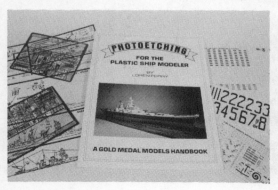

The most significant development for the detailer of plastic ship models is the emergence of etched metal parts, notably those by Loren Perry, who also publishes a useful handbook on their use, and issues some excellent quality decals.

Photoetching for the Plastic Ship Modeller, which shows, by means of some excellent drawings and photographs, how to use these fittings to the best advantage.

Painting ship models

In terms of availability, there are so many excellent ranges of paints, both enamels and acrylics, that there is no problem in finding a make to suit the purpose. It is a matter of how to apply a process that will make or mar the end result. The choice is between traditional brushes and airbrushes. Except for the relatively large areas of hulls and decks, it is doubtful if there is any advantage in using an airbrush at all. When using a brush, a good one should be chosen, a sable or at least a synthetic brush being the best choice. The paint should be applied in several thin coats, never in one thick one. At 1 : 700 scale, paint thickness is important. Too heavy an application will clog fine details and not do justice to your workmanship.

A sequence of painting that follows the logical assembly sequence should be chosen. Break this sequence down into the main hull/deck assembly (paint this as one assembly), and a series of sub-assemblies, each painted and put aside as it is completed. The model can then be carefully assembled, using touches of liquid cement, from the individual sub-assemblies.

Plan the painting. It is obviously easier to paint the decks at this stage rather than later.

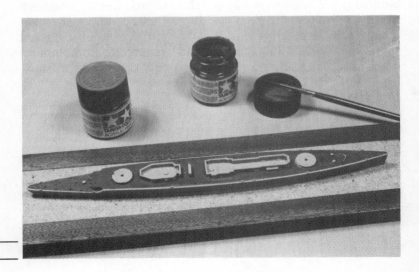

In the final stage, the clean appearance can be toned down by the use of weathering powders—soot around the funnel area for example.

When the major structure of the ship has been completed in this way, the final details can be added. It is possible to paint these carefully, and touch up any faults in this final stage. The decals may be added just before, or just after this point, depending upon the access that is possible. As far as handling during painting is concerned, it will usually be easier for a waterline model to be stuck to its base first.

Having painted the model, some weathering will usually make it look more realistic but it shouldn't be overdone. The best way to do it these days is with Carr's 'weathering powders', which can be bought in any good model railway shop.

Some useful references

A Modeller's Guide to Rigging by A. Richard Mansir, published 1981 by Moonraker Publications.

Lusci's Ship Model Builder's Handbook by Vincenzo Lusci, published in 1970 in Florence with later English translation.

Period Model Boat Manual by F.D. Conte, published in Turin with English translation.

The above three books contain much information on rigging as well as traditional ship modelling. They were recently available from *Maritime Models* of Greenwich.

The Techniques of Ship Modelling by Gerald A. Wingrove, published by Model and Allied Publications, 1974.